Anni Albers

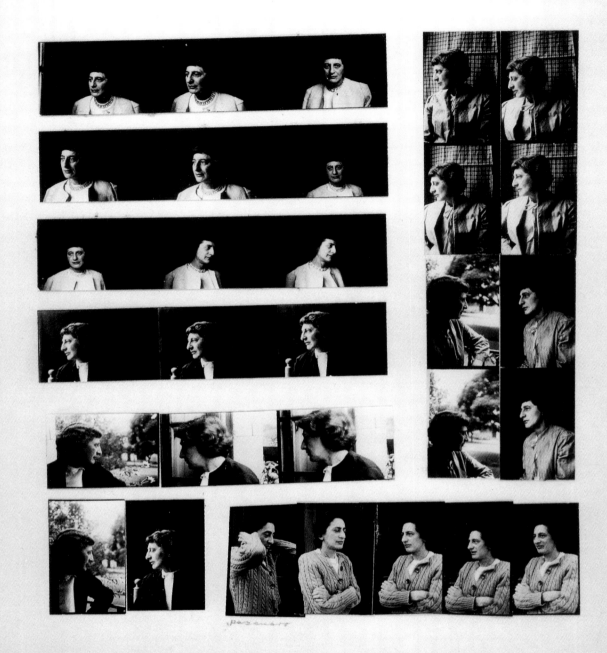

Anni Albers

Nicholas Fox Weber and Pandora Tabatabai Asbaghi

GUGGENHEIM MUSEUM

Published on the occasion of
the exhibition *Anni Albers*,
organized by Nicholas Fox Weber
and Pandora Tabatabai Asbaghi

Peggy Guggenheim Collection, Venice,
    March 24–May 24, 1999
Josef Albers Museum, Bottrop,
    June 12–August 29, 1999
Musée des Arts Décoratifs, Paris,
    September 20–December 31, 1999
The Jewish Museum, New York,
    February 27–June 4, 2000

Front cover
Drapery material, ca. 1944. Commissioned
by Philip Johnson for Rockefeller guest
house, New York. Plastic, copper foil, and
cotton, 99 × 90.5 cm (39 × 35 ⅛ inches).
The Metropolitan Museum of Art, New
York, Gift of Anni Albers 1970.75.10a.

Back cover
Anni Albers at Black Mountain College,
near Asheville, North Carolina, 1947,
photographed by Nancy Newhall.

Frontispiece
Josef Albers, *Pazcuaro*, date unknown.
Collage of twenty contact prints,
mounted on cardboard, 25.4 × 20.3 cm
(10 × 8 inches). The Josef and Anni Albers
Foundation, Bethany JAF:PH-553.

ISBN 0-89207-218-0 (softcover)
ISBN 0-8109-6923-8 (hardcover)

Guggenheim Museum Publications
1071 Fifth Avenue
New York, NewYork 10128

Hardcover edition distributed by
Harry N. Abrams
100 Fifth Avenue
New York, New York 10011

Design: Nathan Garland
Production: Esther Yun
Editor: Jennifer Knox-White

The operations and programs of the Peggy Guggenheim Collection are supported by:

INTRAPRESÆ COLLEZIONE GUGGENHEIM

Aermec
Arclinea
Automotive Products Italia
Banca Antoniana Popolare Veneta
Barbero 1891
Bisazza
DLW AG
Gretag Imaging Group
Gruppo 3M Italia
Gruppo Imation Italia

iGuzzini Illuminazione
Istituto Poligrafico e Zecca dello Stato
Leo Burnett
Lubiam 1911
Luciano Marcato
Rex Built-In
Sàfilo Group
Swatch
Wella
Zucchi – Bassetti Group

Management by Bondardo Comunicazione

The trustees of the Solomon R. Guggenheim Foundation gratefully
acknowledge the Regione Veneto for the annual subsidy that assures the effective
operation of the Peggy Guggenheim Collection.

Official carrier **Alitalia**

Contents

9   Introduction
    Nicholas Fox Weber

28   Thread as Text:
     The Woven Work of Anni Albers
     Virginia Gardner Troy

64   On the Structure
     of the Weavings
     Jean-Paul Leclercq

94   Constructing Textiles
     Anni Albers

118 Anni Albers:
     Devotion to Material
     Kelly Feeney

124 The Last Bauhausler
     Nicholas Fox Weber

152 Anni Albers 1899–1994
     Pandora Tabatabai Asbaghi

Preface

Thomas Krens
Director,
The Solomon R. Guggenheim
Foundation

The Solomon R. Guggenheim Foundation is proud to present the first retrospective of the art of Anni Albers to be shown in Europe, and to do so in the centenary year of her birth. Her little-known story and her art, which is often overshadowed by that of her husband, Josef, belong firmly in the fabric of twentieth-century Modernism, like a thread in one of her weavings. It is a remarkably pure but lively and humane story, touched by some of the dramatic events that took place in Germany between the two world wars and her emigration to a strange land, the United States.

This exhibition has been made possible above all by the Josef and Anni Albers Foundation and by its indefatigable director, Nicholas Fox Weber, who, with Pandora Tabatabai Asbaghi, organized this exhibition. While thanking them personally for their leadership of the project, I also want to acknowledge how full a partnership with the Albers Foundation this exhibition has been. The Albers Foundation has generously made loans from its collections and has contributed the time and unmatchable expertise of its excellent staff. This is not the first time that the Guggenheim Foundation has had the pleasure of working with the Albers Foundation. Our previous collaborations include two highly successful and distinguished exhibitions of the work of Josef Albers, a full retrospective, which originated in 1988 at the Solomon R. Guggenheim Museum in New York, as well as a show devoted to his works in glass, which was shown at the Peggy Guggenheim Collection in Venice in 1994 and at the Solomon R. Guggenheim Museum in New York in 1995. Furthermore, we owe the presence of important paintings and photographs by Josef Albers in the Guggenheim's collections to the extraordinary generosity of the Albers Foundation.

My particular gratitude goes to two New York institutions, the Metropolitan Museum of Art and the Museum of Modern Art, both of which have made many important loans; the cooperation of their professional staffs was vital to the success of this presentation. To the many other lenders to the exhibition, who are listed individually elsewhere in this catalogue, I wish to express my most sincere thanks.

After it closes in Venice, the exhibition will travel to the Josef Albers Museum in Bottrop, Germany, the Musée des Arts Décoratifs in Paris, and the Jewish Museum in New York. It is an honor for the Guggenheim Foundation to be working with these museums, and in particular with Ulrich Schumacher, Marie-Claude Beaud, and Norman Kleeblatt and his colleague Susan Chevlowe at those institutions.

Exhibitions presented at the Peggy Guggenheim Collection are inconceivable without all those who generously provide annual funds for its activities, as is gratefully noted elsewhere. For many years, Alitalia has been the Peggy Guggenheim Collection's official airline; the Regione Veneto has provided an annual subsidy since 1981; the loyal and enthusiastic Advisory Board of the Peggy Guggenheim Collection, presently led by Luigi Moscheri, has been a key part of the collection's success in the eighteen years since it joined the Guggenheim Foundation; and finally, the Intrapresæ Collezione Guggenheim, numbering twenty distinguished European corporations, earmark their annual support specifically to the cultural programs of the collection. Thank you to them all.

Acknowledgments

Nicholas Fox Weber
Executive Director,
The Josef and Anni Albers
Foundation

How appropriate that this major retrospective exhibition, the most complete show ever of Anni Albers's art, which has been organized in honor of the hundredth anniversary of the artist's birth, should have been initiated by the Peggy Guggenheim Collection. Like Anni Albers, Peggy Guggenheim was a perpetual explorer and adventurer, someone who broke down barriers and left behind the potential ease of one sort of existence for the supreme pleasures, as well as the never-ending challenges, of a life devoted to art. It is thanks to the extraordinary steward of Peggy's legacy, the engaged and engaging Philip Rylands, Deputy Director of the Peggy Guggenheim Collection, that this show has been made possible and that it opens in Venice. We feel profound gratitude to him for his vision and his perpetual clarity of thought. At the Peggy Guggenheim, we are also grateful to Renata Rossani, Chiara Barbieri, Beate Barner, Claudia Rech, and Sandra Divari, who have undertaken a range of responsibilities with tremendous grace and energy.

The subsequent venues are equally fitting. The Josef Albers Museum in Bottrop, Germany, is both the great showcase for the art of Anni's husband and partner of fifty years and a kunsthalle for the finest abstract art of the century, under the expert guidance of its director, the splendid and patient Ulrich Schumacher. Then on to the Musée des Arts Décoratifs in Paris, time and again the place where the distinction of craft and art has been rendered nil and where originality and brilliance have been brought to the fore. It is because of its director, the exuberant, perceptive, and tenacious Marie-Claude Beaud—a woman one is certain Anni, however particular in her personal preferences, would have loved—that this exhibition fills that splendid place, with its success assured by Anne de Rougement, Director of Development; Dominique Pallut, Exhibitions Department Manager; and Jean-Paul Leclercq, conservateur en chef du patrimoine chargé des collections antérieures au XIXe siècle. And finally the Jewish Museum in New York, once the home of Edward M. M. Warburg, the patron who, quietly and in the background, paid the Alberses' steamship fare to the United States in the harrowing period after the Gestapo padlocked the doors of the Bauhaus. Thirty years later, it was the farsighted institution that, thanks to the patronage of Vera List, awarded Anni her most significant commission, for the elegiac and powerful *Six Prayers*. Norman Kleeblatt, Susan and Elihu Rose Curator of Fine Arts, and Susan Chevlowe, Associate Curator of Fine Arts, are the open-minded and spirited individuals whom we have to thank for 1109 Fifth Avenue again being Anni's sanctuary in America.

At each of those institutions the support staff has tackled this project with flair and devotion that has made every stage of the work a pleasure. Equal thanks go to those at the Museum of Modern Art and Metropolitan Museum of Art in New York, without whom this project would not have been possible. At the Museum of Modern Art, one must thank, in the Department of Architecture and Design, Matilda McQuaid, Associate Curator; Luisa Lorch, Cataloguer; and Lynda Zycherman, Associate Conservator; at the Metropolitan Museum of Art, Jane Adlin, Curatorial Assistant, Department of Twentieth Century Decorative Arts; and at the Antonio Ratti Textile Center of the Metropolitan Museum, Nobuko Kajitani, Conservator in Charge, and Elena Phipps, Conservator

Gae Aulenti—so alert to Anni's vision; like Anni, so focused on design that is "anonymous and timeless" rather than any attempt to push herself forward; so thorough and quietly assured—is responsible not only for the appearance of this show, but for many of its underlying precepts. Gae's office staff has been wonderful. In particular, we owe profuse thanks to the architect Massimiliano Caruso, who has managed the inordinately complex details of textile presentation with infinite patience and diligence, and to the architect Francesca Fenaroli, for her continuous strength and professionalism.

Pandora Tabatabai Asbaghi, co-curator of this exhibition, sculpted the breadth and depth of its contents, and expanded its concept to include Anni's persona along with her art. Pandora has done so with flair and insight, with the "open eyes" so cherished by both Josef and Anni, and with rare energy and imagination. In compiling the chronology, Tirso Eduard Wiegel provided Pandora with much-appreciated administrative assistance.

Nathan Garland, the designer of this book, has seen, with spectacular conscientiousness and attentiveness, to the creation of a publication that functions, we hope, not only as an exhibition catalogue but as the first volume to approach Anni Albers in adequate range. He was ably assisted by Gregg Chase and Karin Krochmal. Katharine Weber, as editor of some of the text, has tackled difficult tasks with acuity and great finesse.

Great thanks also go to Anthony Calnek, Director of Publications at the Guggenheim, for his superb guidance and constant patience and good humor in overseeing the many stages of assembling this publication in all its complexity. I am also grateful to Elizabeth Levy, Managing Editor/Manager of Foreign Editions; Jennifer Knox-White; Esther Yun, Assistant Production Manager; and Liza Donatelli, Administrative and Editorial Assistant.

Brenda Danilowitz, chief curator of the Josef and Anni Albers Foundation, has, more than anyone else, made this undertaking a reality. Her attention to detail has been nothing short of staggering, her thoroughness and alertness, even under circumstances of intense pressure, amazing. It is impossible to enumerate the tasks she accomplished with fortitude and care, quite simply, this show would not have been possible without her.

Others on the staff of the Albers Foundation have also played essential roles. Jackie Ivy, our curatorial associate, has helped in myriad ways, and specifically in the imaginative and effective presentation of Anni's personal effects. Craig Taylor, curatorial assistant, and Terry Tabaka, building superintendent, have been inordinately helpful in seeing to vital details pertaining to the care of the objects. Phyllis Fitzgerald, our administrative assistant, has, with her professionalism, as well as the history of her long friendship with Anni, been an invaluable support. Camilla Lyons, an intern, did considerable research for the catalogue chronology.

Kelly Feeney, for many years a curator at the foundation, was responsible not only for a re-organization of our Anni Albers holdings and documentation, but also for our success in re-locating, and re-acquiring missing or lost weavings; having known and admired Anni over a long period of time, she did this, and much else, with intense personal devotion and insight. Sarah Lowengard, the textile conservator, has cared for the objects themselves with consummate professionalism and skill and provided essential advice with utmost wisdom and generosity.

Bobbie Dreier, the dearest of friends to both Anni and Josef Albers from the moment of their arrival in America in November of 1933, has done more for this show than she can imagine. She has unearthed some of Anni's most thrilling hardware jewelry as well as other of the artist's splendid handmade objects, provided reminiscences both telling and amusing, and, as always, brought true joy to all of us engaged in Anni's work and life.

I am also grateful in countless ways to my fellow directors of the Albers Foundation, John Eastman and Charles Kingsley, for their unflagging support and generosity. And Anni's brother, Hans Farman, has, as always, been an angel who has provided what no one else could have supplied.

As Anni declared in her favorite quotation from Kandinsky, there is always an "and." On behalf of one of the true pioneers of the twentieth century, of a woman whose integrity was on a par with her talent, and of a wonderful friend, I repeat the words Anni Albers loved to utter more than any others, be it at ceremonial occasions or everyday moments: thank you.

Introduction

Nicholas Fox Weber

Why Anni Albers?

To begin with, she transformed textiles as an art form. Anni elevated the status of woven threads and put the medium on equal footing with oil on canvas and watercolor on paper. And so Buckminster Fuller declared, "Anni Albers, more than any other weaver, has succeeded in exciting mass realization of the complex structure of fabrics. She has brought the artist's intuitive sculpturing faculties and the agelong weaver's arts into historical successful marriage."[1]

She took up weaving reluctantly. Anni had wanted to be a painter, a full-fledged artist, just like the men who attended the Bauhaus around her, but circumstances and certain unalterable realities of her milieu got in the way. Yet even though she felt that she had been forced into textiles, she did her utmost to achieve with the medium what her heroes like Paul Klee and Vasily Kandinsky had accomplished in paint. A pioneer of abstract art when it was still a radical concept, in the 1920s, she made wall hangings of incomparable power and flair and visual excitement. If weavers of previous generations had replicated the flower patterns and decorative motifs that were prescribed for the form, Anni used her yarns to create "visual resting places" (a term she borrowed from one of her heroes, Wilhelm Worringer), which are as calming and diverting as they are infinitely rich and complex. Anni's textile compositions put in visual form aspects of the natural world and of philosophical thought that reflected her endlessly probing, inventive mind.

The direct effects and echoes of her daring search have been far-reaching. Abstract wall hangings have come to flourish as an art form. It has become completely acceptable for thread to be its own voice, to have no obligation to represent anything other than itself. And in her own, extremely small body of work, she made individual masterpieces— weavings that inspire meditation as well as a quick fix, that profoundly enrich the lives of their viewers.

And what a brave woman Anni was! She left the comforts of her luxurious bourgeois upbringing to join those daring souls who wanted to do the unprecedented at the Bauhaus. She married a man from the other side of the tracks—in part because they shared a consuming faith in art. Their joint pursuit of technical and aesthetic heights counted more to them than anything else in life; the visual came both to embody and to represent to them the highest moral and human standards. The making of art was the means and the goal that enabled this wonderful couple not just to survive, but also to thrive, in spite of the sometimes desperate vicissitudes of their existence, in which Nazism, illness, and financial duress were a reality. Their accomplishments triumphed.

Anni's marriage to Josef Albers is, of course, part of the fascination that she holds for us. Neither of them bought into any of the clichés that others might have tried to promulgate on the subject. Sometimes Anni would assume the role of downtrodden wife, but then she would disparage the progress potentially offered by feminism. On the issue of who influenced whom, there is no single answer—except that both were believers in the same cause. Integrity, hard work, the serenity and strength afforded by art at its best, the deliberate avoidance of those sides of the art world that might distract them from their ongoing and diligent search, the mutual loathing of trendiness and corrupt values: this was what the Alberses cared for.

Not only did Anni create individual objects that hold up against some of the finest abstract paintings of the century, but she made functional materials of incomparable subtlety and richness as well as practical

1. Anni Albers, Dessau, ca. 1929, photographed by Umbo.

2. Josef and Anni Albers, Oberstdorf, Germany, 1927–28.

3. Anni and Josef Albers, 1942, photographed by Ted Dreier.

effectiveness. A wall covering she made for an auditorium—the piece that earned her a Bauhaus diploma—was sound-absorbing and light-reflecting while unimaginably modern and soothing to look at. The air and light that flowed through a space divider she designed were as essential to the piece as its wooden strips, dowel, and thread. Another wall covering concealed nail holes. And in all of this the machine and handweaving were extolled equally; the synthetic was revered alongside the natural. Anni's approach was forever original, based more on her own observations and understanding than on anything in the air, and she was wonderfully able to surprise us.

Anni's influence was vast. She directly affected her students at two of the greatest art institutions of the twentieth century—the Bauhaus in Weimar and Dessau, and Black Mountain College near Asheville, North Carolina—and, through her work and writing and the dissemination of her thoughts worldwide, she inspired and guided a large number of artists in directions that have now become part of the mainstream.

And quite late in life she became a printmaker who, in collaboration with some of the leading technicians of the medium, blended screenprint with photo-offset, used the processes of etching, shifted and overprinted plates, and drenched lithographic stones in acid, in such startling and original ways that time and again she achieved the unprecedented, while making art that is as fascinating and engaging as it was brave.

No wonder she so often quoted Kandinsky's, "There is always an 'and.'" That verity certainly applied to her.

And what a writer and aesthetic philosopher she was. Her book *On Designing* invariably has readers exclaiming on its strength and eloquence. Her cultured and educated voice, nourished as it was by the wisdom and temperance of the Enlightenment and Goethe, was infused with a Zen-like reticence and modesty. "The good designer is the anonymous designer, so I believe, the one who does not stand in the way of the material; who sends his products on their way to a useful life without an ambitious appearance. A useful object should perform its duty without much ado."[2] (What would she have made of today's obsession with designers' logos and the conspicuous display of designers' names?) Her faith in art, and the encapsulation of its possibilities, was nothing short of marvelous.

> *The reality of nature will appear to us as never ending. As we examine it, it is endless. It obeys laws never totally lucid to our understanding.*
>
> *The reality of art is concluded in itself. It sets up its own laws as completion of vision.*
>
> *Art is constant and it is complete.*[3]

Who else has articulated such ideas as succinctly or engagingly?

1. Quoted on back jacket of Anni Albers, *On Designing* (Middletown, Conn.: Wesleyan University Press, 1959).
2. "Design: Anonymous and Timeless" (1946), in ibid., pp. 6–7.
3. "Art—A Constant" (1939), in ibid., pp. 47–48.

4. Wall hanging, 1924.
 Cotton and silk, 169.6 × 100.3 cm
(66 13/16 × 39 ½ inches).
The Josef and Anni Albers
Foundation, Bethany.

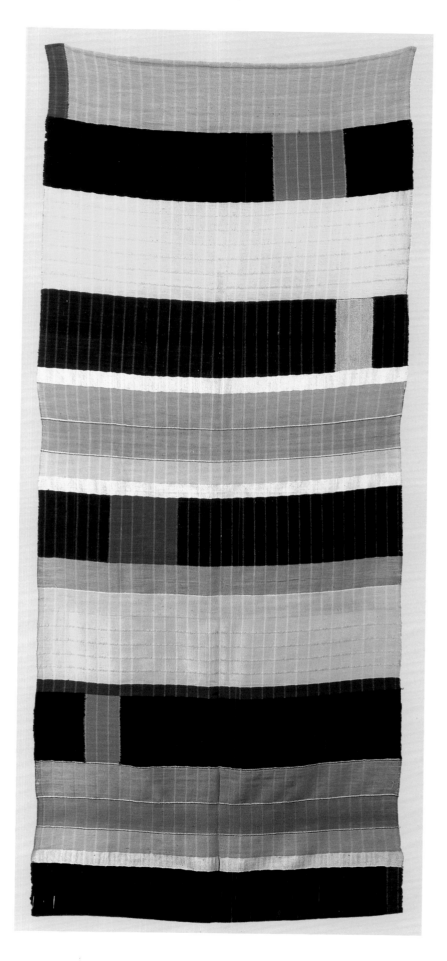

5. Wall hanging, 1925.
Wool and silk, 236 × 96 cm
(92 ⅞ × 37 ¹³⁄₁₆ inches).
Die Neue Sammlung Staatliches
Museum für angewandte Kunst,
Munich 364/26.

6. Wall hanging, 1925.
Silk, cotton, and acetate,
145 × 92 cm (57 ⅛ × 36 ³⁄₁₆ inches).
Die Neue Sammlung Staatliches
Museum für angewandte Kunst,
Munich 363/26.

7. Wall hanging, 1926. Silk,
182.9 × 122 cm (72 × 48 inches).
The Busch-Reisinger Museum,
Harvard University Art Museums,
Cambridge, Massachusetts,
Association Fund BR 48.132.

8. Preliminary design for a wall
hanging, 1926. Gouache and pencil
on paper, 34.9 × 29.5 cm
(13 ¾ × 11 ⅝ inches). The Museum
of Modern Art, New York,
Gift of the designer 397.51.

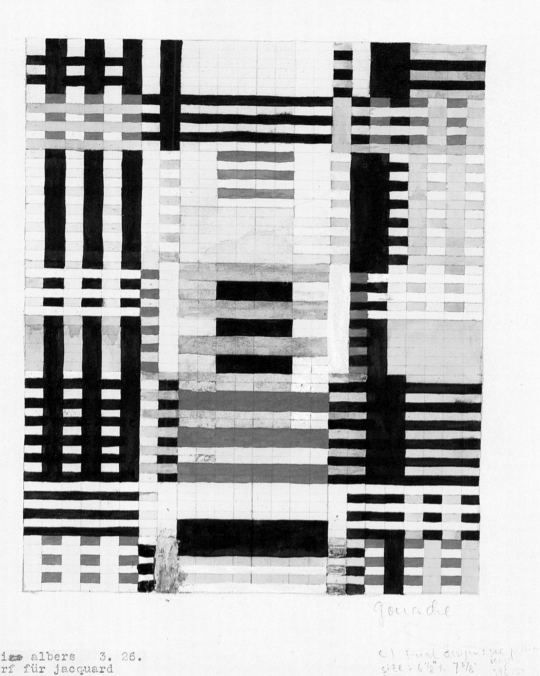

annelise albers   3. 26.
entwurf für jacquard
1.

gouache

9. Preliminary design for a wall
hanging, 1926. Gouache and pencil
on paper, 25.4 × 20.3 cm
(10 × 8 inches). The Museum of
Modern Art, New York,
Gift of the designer 398.51.

10. Design for a jacquard weaving,
1926. Watercolor and gouache
on paper, 34.3 × 28.6 cm
(13 ½ × 11 ¼ inches).
The Busch-Reisinger Museum,
Harvard University Art Museums,
Cambridge, Massachusetts,
Gift of Anni Albers 48.46.

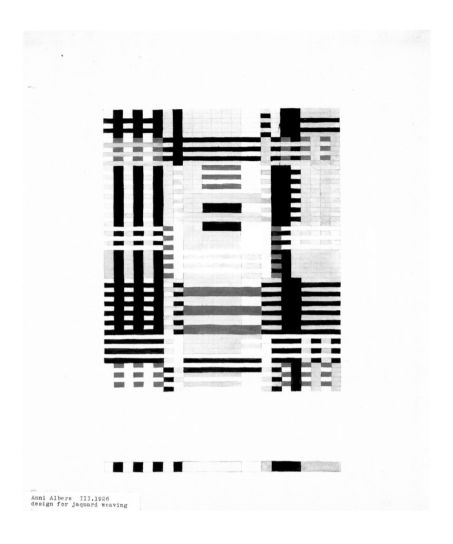

Anni Albers III.1926
design for jaquard weaving

11. Drapery material, 1927.
Designed for the Theater Café Altes,
Dessau. Spun silk, 7 × 105.4 cm
(2 ¼ × 41 ½ inches). The Museum
of Modern Art, New York,
Gift of the designer 451.51.

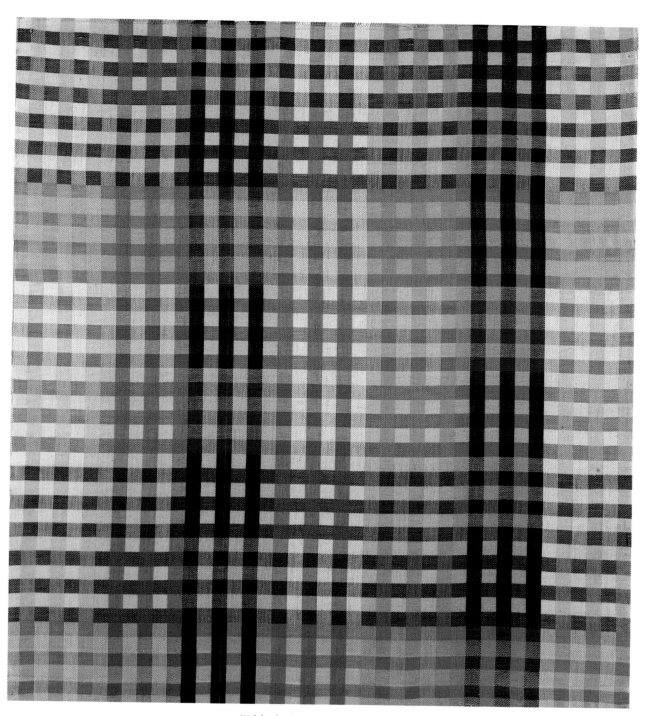

12. Tablecloth material, 1930.
Mercerized cotton, 59.3 × 72.4 cm
(23 ⅜ × 28 ½ inches).
The Museum of Modern Art,
New York, Purchase Fund 561.53.

13. Design for a wall hanging, 1925.
Gouache on paper,
31.7 × 19.2 cm (12½ × 7 9/16 inches).
The Museum of Modern Art, New York,
Gift of the designer 395.51.

annelise albers 12. 27.
jute-teppich *jute rug*
2oo cm. br.
2

not executed

watercolor, india ink

Sizes: 8⅝ × 11" – sketch
        10⅛ × 13⅝ – paper

14. Design for a jute rug, 1927.
Watercolor and india ink on paper,
34.6 × 26.3 cm (13⅛ × 10⅜ inches).
The Museum of Modern Art, New York,
Gift of the designer 403.51.

15. Design for a rug for a child's
room, 1928. Gouache on paper,
34.1 × 26.5 cm (13 ⁷⁄₁₆ × 10 ⁷⁄₁₆ inches).
The Museum of Modern Art,
New York, Gift of the designer
405.51.

watercolor, 1928

Design for bed spread

annelise albers 2. 28.
entwurf für eine bettdecke

size:
inside, 6 7/8" x 8 7/8
outside 10 1/4 x 12 3/4

16. Design for a bedspread, 1928.
Watercolor and pencil on paper,
32.5 × 25.9 cm (12 13/16 × 10 3/16 inches).
The Museum of Modern Art,
New York, Gift of the designer
406.51.

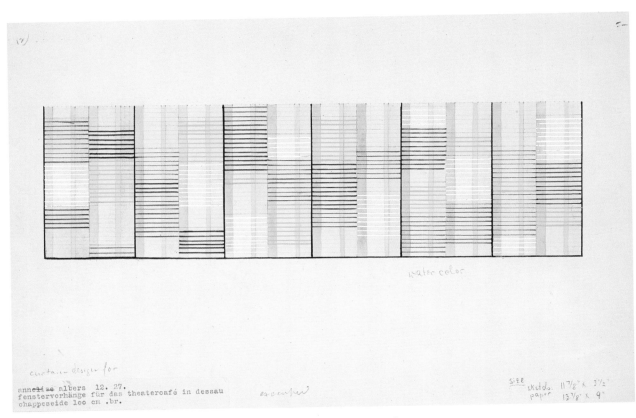

annelise albers 12. 27.
fenstervorhänge für das theatercafé in dessau
chappeseide loo cm .br.

17. Design for drapery material, 1927.
Designed for the Theater Café Altes,
Dessau. Watercolor on paper,
22.9 × 35.2 cm (9 × 13 ⅞ inches).
The Museum of Modern Art, New York,
Gift of the designer 404.51.

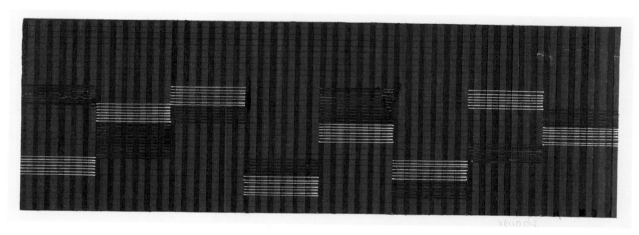

18. Design for a theater curtain,
1928. Gouache on paper,
11.4 × 35.2 cm (4½ × 13⅞ inches).
The Museum of Modern Art,
New York, Gift of the designer
407.51.

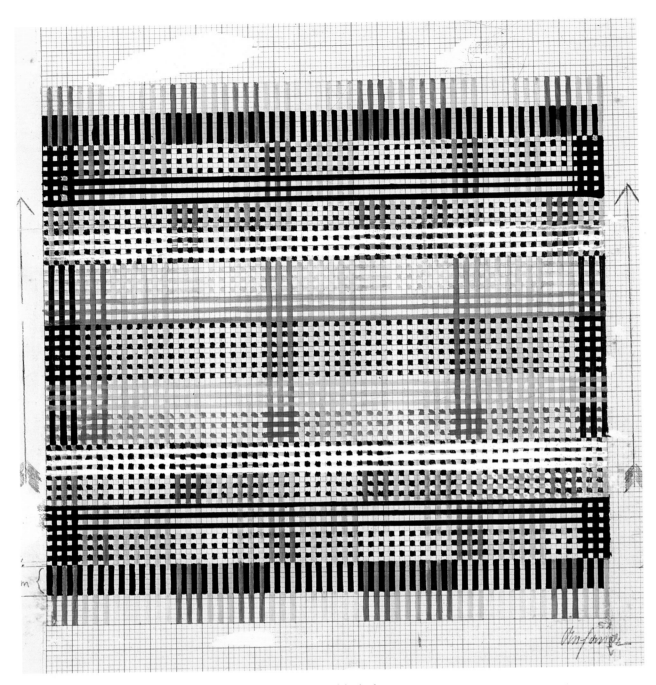

19. Design for a tablecloth, 1930.
Watercolor and gouache
on square-ruled paper,
26 × 24.1 cm (10¼ × 9½ inches).
The Museum of Modern Art,
New York, Gift of the designer
393.51.

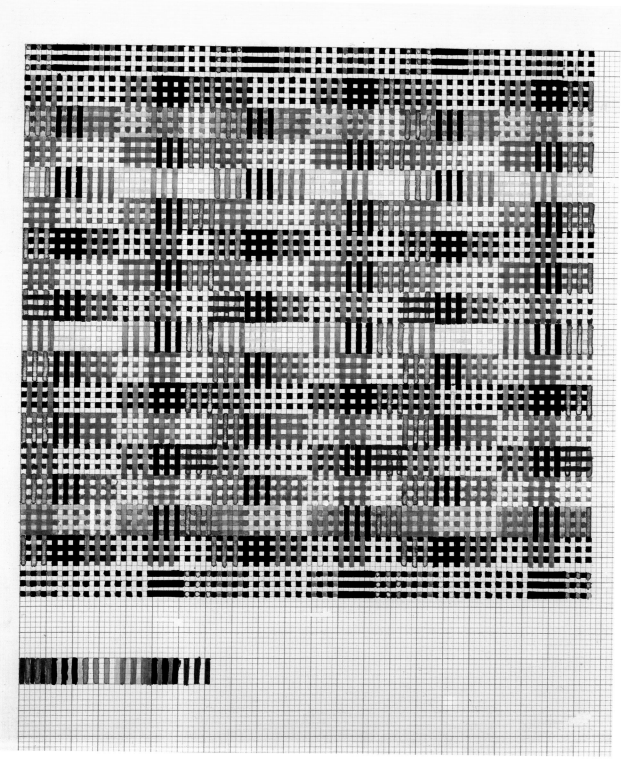

20. Design for a tablecloth, 1930.
Gouache on paper,
30.2 × 23.8 cm (11 ⅞ × 9 ⅜ inches).
The Museum of Modern Art,
New York, Gift of the designer
408.51.

Thread as Text:
The Woven Work of Anni Albers

Virginia Gardner Troy

Anni Albers was acutely aware of the semantic function of thread and textiles in the context of art and design. Throughout her prolific and lengthy weaving career she explored the notion of thread as text to a degree that remains unsurpassed by any other textile artist this century. She achieved this position by synthesizing what she had learned from two primary sources: Andean textiles and the art and teaching of Paul Klee.[1] Albers advanced Andean textiles as "the most outstanding examples of textile art,"[2] calling the weavers of ancient Peru her "great teachers"[3] and using their extraordinary textiles as her primary textbook in her quest to create art that could be "turn[ed] to again and again and that might possibly last for centuries as some ancient Peruvian things have."[4] Of Klee, she stated, "I come always back to Klee as my great hero," because "his art is lasting, and that is what interests me: the lasting things, and not [the] quick passing things."[5] It is significant that Albers linked her great teachers, the Andean weavers, to her hero, Klee, by way of her concept of artistic permanence.

Klee's art and Andean weavings were also connected in Albers's mind by her interest in artistic language. Through her continuous investigation of thread as a *carrier of meaning*, not simply as a utilitarian product, she was able to create art that functions as a visual language, as she believed her ancient Andean predecessors had done.[6] She also embedded her work with poetic content by exploring in thread the notion of the pictograph (a sign or mark that refers to an external subject), the calligraph (a beautiful mark that stands for a letter or word), and the ideograph (a sign that indicates an idea, not necessarily through pictorial representation). These semantic and artistic elements were forms of visual signs that Klee had examined in his art.

Albers's first weavings to result from her interest in visual sign languages were her large, multi-weave wall hangings from the Dessau Bauhaus period, such as an untitled hanging from 1926 (fig. 4), *Black-White-Red* (1926, fig. 21), and *Black-White-Gray* (1927, fig. 22).[7] By this time she had become an important force in leading the Bauhaus's weaving workshop toward a systematic and orderly approach to textile design and production that emphasized the integral relationship between construction and pattern. In this way textiles could be produced in series, and the substitution of one fiber for another, or one weave construction for another, could change the entire nature of the finished textile. At the same time Albers promoted the role of handweaving as one of the first steps of the production process.[8] The use of a system implies the availability of a code to decipher it; in Albers's case the textile itself served as the code, or prototype, for production. The approach to textile design and production that she developed at the Bauhaus was one of Albers's great achievements,

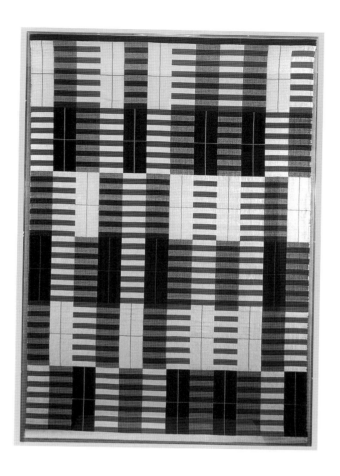

21. *Black-White-Red*, 1964
reconstruction of a 1926 original.
Cotton and silk, 175 × 118 cm
(68 ⅞ × 46 ⁷⁄₁₆ inches).
Bauhaus-Archiv, Berlin.

22. *Black-White-Gray*, 1964
reconstruction of a 1927 original.
Cotton and silk, 147 × 118 cm
(57 ⅞ × 46 ⁷⁄₁₆ inches).
Bauhaus-Archiv, Berlin.

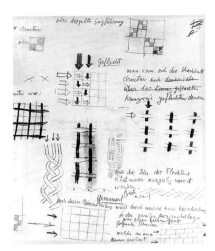

23. Paul Klee, Page from the "Pädagogischen Nachlass," ca. 1923. Kunstmuseum Bern, Paul Klee Stiftung.

24. *Tocapu* tunic, Island of Titicaca, found in a stone chest near Moro-Kato. American Museum of Natural History, New York, Part of the Garces Collection, Purchased by A. F. Bandelier in 1896 32601.

for it provided an alternative to the narrative and figural European tapestry tradition—in which a textile was produced by weavers based on cartoons often created by others—and it allowed the modern weaver to compose directly on the loom.[9] Through her study of Andean textiles, Albers was able to understand how the direct communication between use and design, between process and product, was accomplished in ancient times on simple hand looms by a sophisticated culture that did not use conventional Western writing systems, but instead employed symbols to communicate ideas.[10]

In designing her wall hangings, Albers employed a system based on a language of geometric, modular forms, which she arranged according to the principles of rotation, color swapping, repetition, multiplication, and division. These principles, which Klee taught in his theoretical classes at the Bauhaus, had an integral relationship to the underlying structure of weaving. The year 1927 was an important one for Albers, because she was among those who attended a course taught by Klee specifically for weaving-workshop students.[11] Certainly she had had access to his work before this time through his published pedagogical notebooks and exhibitions of his work.[12] "We were so full of admiration for Klee," she once stated,[13] and later added, "He was my god at the time."[14] What she primarily absorbed from Klee during his course were his lessons dealing with structural composition, particularly in relation to the grid. As Klee explained it, the grid is a structure generated both by the repetition of units as well as by the under- and overlapping of bands. Pages from his pedagogical notebooks show that weaving featured in his thoughts on the grid. Indeed, for a unit on structural composition he diagrammed the warp and weft construction of weaving as well as weaving in cross section in order to show the inherent checkerboard pattern of the medium (fig. 23).[15]

"I think I owe most of my insight into problems of form to Klee," Albers later stated, pointing to Klee's importance as a source for her early investigations into the language of nonobjective form and its significance within the idiom of weaving.[16] The geometric patterns that she created within a grid format are essentially self-referential in that they are inherent to the works' structure; at the same time they suggest both the image and the idea of text. The viewer scans the images for clues to a code, and by doing so becomes engaged in a perceptual activity not unlike that of reading.

Albers's exploration of textiles as text through the arrangement of sign modules was reinforced during this period by the Andean textiles she saw in various museums.[17] She admired the dazzling and complex color and shape patterning of Inca, Wari, and Tiawanaku tunics, which have a strong similarity to the type of patterning she was exploring at the Bauhaus. She also studied Andean open-weave and multi-weave textiles. Albers responded primarily to the concept and use of ideographic signs and structures in these textiles rather than to specific iconography, even though she was aware that discrete information about the Andean world was embedded within their forms and structures. She was particularly interested in the Inca tunics that incorporated a geometric motif patterning known as *tocapu* in the Quechua language. She would have seen outstanding examples of such tunics in the Museum für Völkerkunde in Berlin and Munich,[18] as well as in two books: Walter Lehmann's *Kunstgeschichte des Alten Peru* (1923, fig. 24) and Raoul d'Harcourt's *Les Tissus Indiens du Vieux Pérou* (1924).[19] These technically extraordinary, handmade textiles, with their complex geometric and color arrangements, served as ideal formal and technical models for Albers's exploration of textiles as art.

Albers immigrated to the United States with her husband, Josef, in 1933. From that year until 1949 she taught at Black Mountain College, near Asheville, North Carolina. In 1935 the couple made the first of more than fourteen trips to Mexico and South America.[20] From the start she combed the markets in Mexico for "old things," including Andean textiles for her personal textile collection. During these trips she also assembled a substantial collection of textiles for Black Mountain College, and acquired numerous items for her and Josef's collection of Mesoamerican and Andean art, which eventually included more than one thousand ceramic, stone, jade, and textile pieces.[21]

The dramatic changes that occurred in Albers's woven work immediately after her first visit to Mexico reflect her deepening understanding of ancient American art. She was also beginning to fully understand the impact of Klee's work and teaching now that she was able to look back upon her Bauhaus years and filter her memories of them. The first two wall hangings she made in the United States, *Ancient Writing* and *Monte Alban* (both 1936, figs. 37 and 38), which are possibly companion pieces, were decisively different from her Bauhaus work. Both pieces incorporate an element of Klee's art that she assimilated in her own work only after her Bauhaus period: the exploration of the personal and associational aspects of subject matter, particularly in the context of semantics.

With *Monte Alban* Albers used for the first time a technique that she practiced throughout her subsequent weaving career: the supplementary, or floating, weft, in which an extra weft thread is threaded, or "floated," above the woven surface. Albers would have seen this common Andean technique—which is still widely used in modern Latin America—in Germany and in publications; indeed, she owned numerous examples of it.[22] In *Monte Alban* Albers used this technique to "draw" lines on the surface of the woven structure to refer to the ascending and descending steps, the flat plazas, and the underground chambers of the ancient site after which the work is named. "We were aware of layer upon layer of former civilization under the ground," she wrote of her visit to the site.[23] The supplementary-weft technique allowed her to devote attention to the *surface* of the weaving. While the structure of the overall textile continued to be vitally important, her focus on the inscription was a significant departure from her Bauhaus work. This change reveals her new understanding of both Andean art and Klee's vision. She later said, "I find that [Klee] probably had . . . influence on my work and my thinking by just looking at what he did with a line or a dot or a brush stroke, and I tried in a way to find my way in my own material and my own craft discipline."[24]

In *Ancient Writing* she similarly used a title and abstract visual forms to imply content. She evoked the idea of visual language by grouping together differently textured and patterned squares like words or glyphs, locking this "text" into an underlying grid. The "text," which is set within margins, appears to jump forward to be "read" like words on a page.[25] Like Klee, Albers sometimes used pictographic, calligraphic, and ideographic signs simultaneously in her work in order to address concerns related to visual language and mark-making, a practice that occupied Albers throughout her career in the United States and that she continually framed within the context of Andean textiles. She was amazed that Andean culture seems to have had no written language, and she concluded that the textile medium itself "was their language . . . their way of speaking about the world."[26]

Monte Alban and *Ancient Writing* signaled the beginning of Albers's long exploration of what she called her "pictorial weaving." This term is somewhat contradictory in that she never wove recognizable pictures in the traditional European manner; "abstract pictorial weaving" (as

25. Quipu, Inca, from the coastal valley of Chancay, Peru. American Museum of Natural History, New York 325190.

opposed to "figurative pictorial weaving") would be a more accurate term. Albers thought of the floating-weft technique as one method by which to create a unique pictorial image in thread as she worked toward "the direction of art."[27] She believed that the creation of art revolved around the process of articulation: "To let threads be articulate again," she wrote, "is the raison d'être of my pictorial weavings."[28]

With the augmentation of the floating-weft thread, which essentially created unique objects of her weavings, Albers could effectively change her work from prototype to art. For her pictorial weaving *Black-White-Gold I* (1950, fig. 42), she added calligraphic floating-weft threads upon the central portion of the woven field. She also introduced the supplementary knotted weft, a technique derived from a Peruvian source, most likely the elaborate Andean recording device called a quipu, a knotted thread instrument that held codified data (see fig. 25).[29] Discussing the Andeans' use of quipus, Albers stated,

> [Andean weavers] developed a very tricky mathematics. . . . These instruments were, again, not written. They didn't have writing, as I told you. But what they did [have] was threads . . . called quipus, this instrument. And the different things that they had to deliver were designated on each thread. The amount was indicated with different knots and different heights and so on. I knew once, at one time, how to do it.[30]

Here was a clear example of thread functioning as text, which Albers innovatively translated and applied to her own work.

Albers's pictorial woven work of the 1950s to the early 1960s was dominated by her interest in and use of visual sign languages. She believed that textiles, particularly Andean textiles, served as "transmitters of meaning." She wrote,

> Along with cave paintings, threads were among the earliest transmitters of meaning. In Peru, where no written language in the generally understood sense had developed even by the time of the conquest in the sixteenth century, we find—to my mind not in spite of this but because of it—one of the highest textile cultures we have come to know.[31]

Albers wove *Two* (fig. 44) in 1952 with these thoughts in mind. On top of an underlying plain-weave checkerboard ground, Albers wove heavy dark fibers using a supplementary technique. Thus the dark shapes appear to overlap one another upon the ground, creating a dynamic and scriptlike figure-ground relationship. *Two* was originally woven "sideways," with the short end in the vertical direction; afterwards Albers turned it horizontally, and signed it on the lower right. The practice of working in one direction and then turning it to another after completion was frequently employed by expert Andean weavers of the Middle Horizon (500–900 AD) and Late Horizon (1438–1534 AD) periods.[32] Klee, too, frequently turned or inverted his work after completion.[33]

Two is a particularly significant and striking piece because of its clear indebtedness to De Stijl. Albers maintained her involvement with the formal vocabulary of De Stijl—which she first learned at the Bauhaus—for over three decades, viewing it in light of her contact with ancient American art. She saw parallels between De Stijl and Andean textiles in their use of universal abstract languages and patterns.[34] Albers was aware that early De Stijl images were essentially distillations of recognizable subject matter—abstractions that resulted in pictographic representations—while later images moved toward the ideographic and the nonobjective. She would also have noticed that Piet Mondrian's and Theo van Doesburg's linear block compositions echo the inherent construction of weaving and create figure-ground relationships like that of text on a page.[35]

The parallels between the principles of De Stijl and Andean textiles are particularly apparent in works in which figure-ground relationships are ambiguous and abstract pictorial signs merge with ideographic ones.[36] Albers owned numerous Andean textiles that contain this visual ambiguity, such as a Chancay fragment constructed with two different techniques: the top portion is supplementary-weft brocade, while the lower portion is interlocked tapestry (fig. 26). Both parts involve dynamic color and value patterning, as well as bold figure-ground relationships that are established through contrast and repetition. In its stepped lines and figure-ground reversals, the lower portion is clearly a formal source for *Two*, while the upper portion served as a technical source.

Two also reveals an indebtedness to Klee's late script pictures with their graffitilike signs, which Albers would have seen at the 1949 Klee retrospective at the Museum of Modern Art.[37] Interestingly, Klee painted many of these late works on burlap, a loosely woven, natural-fiber cloth. When burlap is painted, the warp-and-weft structure and texture of the cloth is emphasized, as in Klee's *Flora on the Rocks* (*Flora am Felsen*, 1940, fig. 27), resulting in a work that appears to be both painting and textile. Klee frequently explored the merging of artistic techniques along with the merging of signs, and Albers clearly emulated this fluid approach.

Soon after Albers made *Two* she wove what may have been a companion piece, *Pictographic* (1953, fig. 28), also a long rectangle woven sideways.[38] Blocks of color arranged on a checkerboard ground are "inscribed" with forty-one *X*s. As in *Two*, Albers used line and shape in this work to refer to the image of a text. While the contrast between light and dark is not as pronounced in *Pictographic* as it is in *Two*, the varying degrees of value and intensity between the blocks and the *X*s produce subtle figure-ground relationships that evoke a passage of text or layers of text.

The most striking examples of Albers's pictorial weavings from the 1950s and 1960s can be divided into two main thematic groups: those using imagery derived from ancient American motifs or landscapes, such as *South of the Border* (1958) and *Tikal* (1958); and those evoking linguistic characters and systems through the rectilinear arrangement of ideographic signs. Many of the titles of these latter works have direct textual references, as in *Memo* (1958), *Open Letter* (1958), *Jotting* (1959), *Haiku* (1961), and *Code* (1962). In light of Albers's focus on inscriptions and signs it is interesting to note that some of the first pieces of ancient American art that Albers purchased in Mexico were ceramic and stone stamps used to print and block designs (figs. 29–32).[39] These stamps are similar to the type once used to compose text in printing in that both require the creation of a figure-ground relationship in order for the image or text to be seen and therefore read.

The relationship of image/text to ground was one that Albers delighted in and explored with increasing intensity during the 1950s. Her pictorial weavings of this period reveal a deliberate effort to create a high degree of contrast between figure and ground, and to maintain a strict rectilinearity within patterns and in pattern sequences. In *Memo,* for example, she employed a repertoire of sign characters that are similar to an alphabet, and these are arranged along horizontal bars. Although one's automatic response is to read this "memo" for information, Albers's intention was not simply to simulate a page of text; rather, she sought to investigate the nature of ideographic signs and the expression of codified visual information through thread.

26. Pre-Columbian textile fragment, Chancay, 1100–1400 AD. Cotton, 16.5 × 12.7 cm (6⅜ × 5 inches). The Anni Albers Collection of Pre-Columbian Textiles of the Josef and Anni Albers Foundation, Bethany.

27. Paul Klee, *Flora on the Rocks* (*Flora am Felsen*), 1940. Oil and tempera on burlap, 90.7 × 70.5 cm (35 ¹¹⁄₁₆ × 27 ¾ inches). Kunstmuseum Bern G 1622.

28. *Pictographic*, 1953. Cotton,
45.7 × 101.6 cm (18 × 40 inches). The
Detroit Institute of Arts, Founders Society
purchase, Stanley and Madalyn Rosen
Fund, Dr. and Mrs. George Kamperman
Fund, Octavia W. Bates Fund, Emma S.
Fechimer and William C. Yawkey Fund.

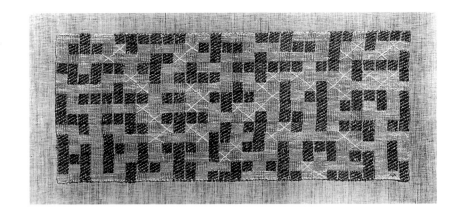

29. Pre-Columbian stamp, Guerrero,
1250–1521 AD. Ceramic, 7 cm (2 ¼ inches)
wide. Peabody Museum of Natural
History, New Haven, Connecticut, Gift of
Josef and Anni Albers 251685.

30. Pre-Columbian stamp, Highland
Mexico, 1250–1521 AD. Ceramic, 8 cm (3 ⅛
inches) wide. Peabody Museum of Natural
History, New Haven, Connecticut, Gift of
Josef and Anni Albers 257022.

31. Pre-Columbian roller stamp, possibly
Valley of Mexico, 1200–100 BC. Perforated
sandstone, 8 cm (3 ⅛ inches) long. Peabody
Museum of Natural History,
New Haven, Connecticut, Gift of Josef
and Anni Albers 257679.

32. Pre-Columbian roller stamp, Tlatilco,
Valley of Mexico, 1200–900 BC. Ceramic,
9 cm (3 ½ inches) long. Peabody Museum
of Natural History, New Haven,
Connecticut, Gift of Josef and Anni Albers
257542.

Play of Squares (1955, fig. 47) also relates significantly to semantics, in a way that has generally been overlooked in discussions of Albers's work: its element of play. Thirty-six white squares and thirty-three dark brown squares appear in apparently random order along twenty-three horizontal bands. As the viewer scans for a code, one system is revealed—every row has either three dark squares on a light brown band or three light squares on a medium brown band—but an overall, sequential formula does not emerge. In this way, *Play of Squares* is similar to Albers's *Black-White-Gray* (1927), but *Play of Squares* is smaller and nubbier in texture than the earlier work, and its title suggests that it is more poetic and improvisational. This nonsensical and apparently random arrangement of squares within a linear format evokes an ambiguous arrangement of words and letters (a play of words) or of musical notes (a play of sounds). Here Albers's connection to Klee is again apparent: Klee, a master of word play, shifting signs, and improvisation, perfected the art of visual punning by skillfully creating figures, shapes, and texts that could metamorphose from one thing to another depending on the viewer's reading of them.

Albers was clearly aware that the strict limitations of the weaving process could easily overwhelm creativity, so she continually advanced the role of improvisation and frequently brought up the subject of play when discussing the creative process. In her 1941 article "Handweaving Today," for example, she suggested that designing at the loom should first involve play:

> An elementary approach will be a playful beginning, unresponsive to any demand of usefulness, an enjoyment of colors, forms, surface contrasts and harmonies, a tactile sensuousness. This first and always most important pleasure in the physical qualities of materials needs but the simplest technique and must be sustained through the most complicated one. For just this satisfaction coming from material qualities is part of the satisfaction we get from art.[40]

Through this playful working with materials, Albers believed that the artist could begin to create meaningful form.

Two main efforts dominated Albers's work of the 1960s: large woven murals for public spaces—primarily ark curtains for synagogues—and her book *On Weaving*, which is still a standard text in weaving courses today. The synagogue commissions required Albers to approach text-related issues in yet another way, and this resulted in powerful ark curtains that both protect and celebrate the Hebrew Scriptures.

Albers achieved the union of art and utility that is evident in these curtains through her admiration and understanding of the work of Klee, who sought to interpret the physical and metaphysical worlds in codified yet playful ways. This union can equally be attributed to her study of Andean textiles. In *On Weaving* she described the work of the Andean weavers with admiration:

> Of infinite phantasy within the world of threads, conveying strength or playfulness, mystery or the reality of their surroundings, endlessly varied in presentation and construction, even though bound to a code of basic concepts, these textiles set a standard of achievement that is unsurpassed.[41]

From these two sources, Albers derived the inspiration for her exploration of semantics within the field of weaving. As a teacher, collector, student, and artist, Albers has inspired subsequent generations of artists and designers to strive to create, like Klee, the Andean weavers, and Albers herself, an art that is lasting and meaningful.

Pre-Columbian textile
fragments from Anni Albers's
personal collection

33. Late Intermediate period
(1100–1400 AD). Cotton and wool,
36.2 × 18.1 cm (14¼ × 7⅛ inches).
The Josef and Anni Albers
Foundation, Bethany PC018.

34. Nasca period (100 BC–700 AD).
Wool, 36.2 × 7.9 cm
(14¼ × 3⅛ inches).
The Josef and Anni Albers
Foundation, Bethany PC032.

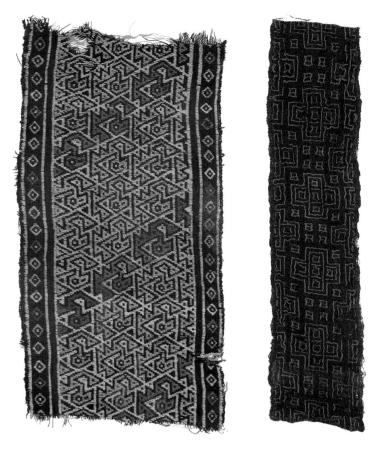

35. Middle Horizon period
(500–900 AD). Cotton and
wool, 27.6 × 30.2 cm
(10⅞ × 11⅞ inches).
The Josef and Anni Albers
Foundation, Bethany PC020.

1. Mary Jane Jacob, in her essay "Anni Albers: A Modern Weaver as Artist," in *The Woven and Graphic Art of Anni Albers* (Washington, D.C.: Smithsonian Press, 1985), was the first to discuss the textual references in Albers's pictorial weavings, and she also briefly mentioned a connection between Albers's open weaves and her contact with Peruvian weaving (p. 72). For further discussion of these topics, see the following essays by Virginia Gardner Troy: "Anni Albers: The Significance of Ancient American Art for Her Woven and Pedagogical Work," Ph.D. diss., Emory University, Atlanta, 1997 (Ann Arbor, Mich.: UMI Publications, 1997); "Anni Albers und die Textilkunst der Anden," in Josef Helfenstein and Henriette Mentha, eds., *Josef und Anni Albers, Europa und Amerika, Künstlerpaare—Künstlerfreunde* (exh. cat.; Bern: Kunstmuseum Bern; Cologne: Dumont, 1998); and "Andean Textiles at the Bauhaus: Awareness and Application," *Surface Design Journal* 20, no. 2 (winter 1996), pp. 10–11, 35–37.

2. Anni Albers, *On Weaving* (Middletown, Conn.: Wesleyan University Press, 1965), pp. 69–70.

3. Ibid., p. 6.

4. Sevim Fesci, interview with Anni Albers, New Haven, Conn., July 5, 1968, Archives of American Art, New York; transcript in The Josef and Anni Albers Foundation archives, p. 5.

5. Richard Polsky, interview with Anni Albers, Orange, Conn., Jan. 11, 1985, "American Craftspeople Project," Oral Research Office, Columbia University, New York; transcript in The Josef and Anni Albers Foundation archives, pp. 49–51.

6. Recent texts that discuss the subject of thread as a social document in terms of ancient American textiles include Jane Schneider, "The Anthropology of Cloth," *Annual Review of Anthropology* 16 (1987), pp. 409–48; Rebecca Stone-Miller, *To Weave for the Sun: Andean Textiles in the Museum of Fine Arts* (Boston: Museum of Fine Arts, 1992); Elizabeth Hill Boone and Walter Mignolo, eds., *Writing Without Words: Alternative Literacies in Mesoamerica and the Andes* (Durham: Duke University Press, 1994); and César Paternosto, *The Stone and the Thread: Andean Roots of Abstract Art*, trans. Esther Allen (Austin: University of Texas Press, 1996).

7. Albers described multiweave constructions within the context of Andean textiles in *On Weaving* (p. 50): "Double weaves are fabrics that have two separate layers which can be locked at both sides, at one side, or, within the fabric, at any number of places where the design asks for an exchange of top and bottom layers, usually of different colors. There are also triple weaves and quadruple weaves. . . . In ancient Peru, double weaves in complicated designs were made, and triple weaves have been found, as well as a small quadruple piece. If a highly intelligent people with no written language, no graph paper, and no pencils could manage such inventions, we should be able—easily I hope—to repeat at least these structures."

8. Recent texts that discuss the weaving workshop at the Bauhaus include Anja Baumhoff, "Gender Art and Handicraft at the Bauhaus," Ph.D. diss., Johns Hopkins University, Baltimore, 1994; Magdalena Droste, *Gunta Stölzl* (Berlin: Bauhaus-Archiv, 1987); Petra Maria Jocks, "Eine Weberin am Bauhaus, Anni Albers, Zwischen Kunst und Leben," Master's thesis, University of Frankfurt am Main, 1986; Ingrid Radewaldt, "Bauhaustextilien 1919–1933," Ph.D. diss., University of Hamburg, 1986; and Sigrid Wortmann Weltge, *Bauhaus Textiles* (London: Thames and Hudson, 1993).

9. In her 1924 article "Bauhausweberei," Albers (who was then known as Annelise Fleischmann) suggested that modern weavers could learn from ancient weavers, who wove "according to the inherent properties of handicraft and material" rather than following prepared plans. "Bauhausweberei," *Junge Menschen* 8 (Nov. 1924), p. 188; reprinted in *Bauhaus Weimar: Sonderheft der Zeitschrift "Junge Menschen"* (Munich: Kraus Reprint, 1980).

10. This was discussed in two important pre–World War I German publications: W. Reiss and A. Stübel, *Das Totenfeld von Ancon* (Berlin, 1880–87), translated into English as *The Necropolis at Ancon in Peru* (London and Berlin: Asher & Co., 1906); and Max Schmidt, "Über Altperuanische Gewebe mit Szenenhaften Darstellungen," in P. Ehrenreich, ed., *Baessler-Archiv: Beiträge zur Völkerkunde*, vol. 1 (Leipzig and Berlin: Teubner Verlag, 1911; New York: Johnson Reprint, 1968). During the Weimar Bauhaus period, these factors were discussed in Ernest Fuhrmann, *Reich der Inka* (Hagen and Darmstadt: Folkwang Museum, 1922); Wilhelm Hausenstein, *Barbaren und Klassiker: ein Buch von der Bildnerei exotischer Volker* (Munich: Piper Verlag, 1922); Herbert Kühn, *Die Kunst der Primitiven* (Munich: Delphin-Verlag, 1923); and Eckart von Sydow, *Die Kunst der Naturvolker und der Vorzeit* (Berlin: Propylaen-Kunstgeschichte, 1923). Albers and other members of the Bauhaus were most likely familiar with all of these books. See Troy, "Anni Albers: The Significance of Ancient American Art for Her Woven and Pedagogical Work," pp. 37–44 and 65–74.

11. Albers joined the Bauhaus in 1922, taking the preliminary course with Georg Muche at that time and then Johannes Itten's course in 1922–23. In 1923, her third semester, she joined the weaving workshop. During her fourth semester, in 1923–24, she assisted in the dye laboratory, and in her fifth semester, in 1924, she most likely completed her first wall hanging. She took Vasily Kandinsky's "theory of form" course during the 1925–26 semester. From September to December 1929, she was acting director of the weaving workshop. After

graduating in 1930 Albers worked independently and again served briefly (during the fall of 1931) as director of the weaving workshop. Droste, *Gunta Stölzl*, pp. 143–55.

12. Albers had purchased Klee's *Two Forces* (*Zwei Kräfte*, 1922) in 1924. The Josef and Anni Albers Foundation generously provided me with this information.

13. Neil Welliver, "A Conversation with Anni Albers," *Craft Horizons*, July–Aug. 1967, p. 15.

14. Nicholas Fox Weber, "Anni Albers to Date," in *The Woven and Graphic Art of Anni Albers*, p. 19.

15. Klee's notes for this lesson, which he titled "Constructive Approaches to Composition," appear in Klee, *Notebooks, Vol. Two: The Nature of Nature*, ed. Jürg Spiller, trans. Heinz Norden (New York: Wittenborn, 1973), p. 241. The lesson is not dated, but it follows his lessons on structure dated Saturday, 10 November 1923, and it is assumed that "Constructive Approaches to Composition" was included in the same series. (The dates of lessons are not always clear in the two published volumes of Klee's notebooks.) Josef and Anni Albers owned a copy of Klee's classroom handbook, *Pädagogisches Skizzenbuch* (published by the Bauhaus in 1925), which included his earlier classroom exercises. The handbook was published in English as *Pedagogical Sketchbook*, ed. Walter Gropius and László Moholy-Nagy, trans. Sibyl Moholy-Nagy (New York: Praeger, 1953).

16. Welliver, "A Conversation with Anni Albers," p. 21.

17. Albers remarked in 1984 that her interest in Pre-Columbian art began in Germany, and that she frequently visited the ethnographic museums there. Nicholas Fox Weber, video interview with Anni Albers, 1984, The Josef and Anni Albers Foundation archives.

18. By 1907, the Museum für Völkerkunde in Berlin already owned more than 7,500 Andean textiles, making it the largest collection of these textiles in Europe at the time. Major donations of Andean art to the museum included the Baessler donation of 11,690 items in 1899 and the Reiss and Stübel donation of 2,000 items in 1879. The museum acquired 2,400 items in 1882 from Dr. José Mariano Macedo of Lima, and subsequently the large Centeno collection from Cuzco in 1888 and the Bolivar collection in 1904. Wilhelm Gretzer sold 27,254 ancient American pieces to the museum in 1907. Immina von Schuler-Schömig, "The Central Andean Collections at the Museum für Völkerkunde, Berlin, Their Origin and Present Organization," in Anne-Marie Hocquenghem, ed., *Pre-Columbian Collections in European Museums* (Budapest: Akademiai Kiado, 1987), pp. 163–65. See also Corinna Raddatz, "Christian Theodor Wilhelm Gretzer and his Pre-Columbian Collection in the Niedersächsisches Landesmuseum of Hannover," in the same

publication (pp. 169–75).

19. Albers used Lehmann's book, as well as Max Schmidt's extensive *Kunst und Kultur von Peru* (1929), when she taught at Black Mountain College, according to former students Don Page and Lore Kadden Lindenfeld and former colleague Tony Landreau. (Letters to the author from Page, Sept. 4, 1996; Lindenfeld, Nov. 20, 1996; and Landreau, Sept. 25, 1996.) Albers's personal slide collection included numerous images from Lehmann's book, as well as images of other Andean textiles, and she owned the 1934 French edition of d'Harcourt. (Much of Albers's library is now held at The Josef and Anni Albers Foundation.) Schmidt's *Kunst und Kultur von Peru* was published by Ullstein; Albers's mother, Toni Ullstein Fleischmann, was a member of this prominent publishing family.

20. A summary of the Alberses' travels follows: 1934, Florida, Havana; 1935, Mexico; 1936, Mexico; 1937, Mexico; 1938, Florida; 1939, Mexico; 1940, Mexico; 1941, Mexico; 1946–47, Mexico, New Mexico; 1949, Mexico; 1952, Mexico, Havana; 1953, Chile, Peru; 1956, Mexico, Peru, Chile; 1962, Mexico; 1967, Mexico. This list was compiled from documents held in the Black Mountain College Papers, North Carolina State Archives, Raleigh, and The Josef and Anni Albers Foundation archives.

21. For information regarding the Alberses' trips to Mexico in 1937 and 1939, see Toni Ullstein Fleischmann's 1937–39 travel diaries; English transcript, translated by Fleischmann's grandson Theodore Benfey, in The Josef and Anni Albers Foundation archives. Anni's mother and father, Toni and Siegfried Fleischmann, met Josef and Anni in Veracruz in 1937 and again in 1939 after fleeing Nazi Germany. The Alberses had three main collections of ancient American art: The Josef and Anni Albers Collection of Pre-Columbian Art, which is now housed at the Peabody Museum, Yale University Art Gallery, and at the Josef and Anni Albers Foundation (see Karl Taube, *The Josef and Anni Albers Collection of Pre-Columbian Art* [New York: Hudson Hills Press, 1988], p. 9, and Anni Albers and Michael Coe, *Pre-Columbian Mexican Miniatures: The Josef and Anni Albers Collection* [New York: Praeger, 1970], p. 4); The Anni Albers Collection of Pre-Columbian Textiles (comprised of 113 Andean textiles), which is now at the Josef and Anni Albers Foundation; and The Harriett Englehardt Memorial Collection of Textiles (comprised of ninety-two textiles purchased by Anni Albers for Black Mountain College), which is now housed at Yale University Art Gallery. Black Mountain College Papers, vol. 2, box 8; and Troy, "Anni Albers: The Significance of Ancient American Art for Her Woven and Pedagogical Work," pp. 163–69.

22. A cotton Chancay in Albers's collection is particularly striking because it is one of

the few fully finished pieces that she owned. It has four finished edges, or selvages, and although it has become somewhat distorted due to wear, is approximately the size of a standard sheet of paper (seven by eleven inches). On it, twenty-five cuttlefish were woven using the supplementary-weft technique. Albers would have appreciated the completeness of this work and the repetition of the fish in grid formation.

23. Albers and Coe, *Pre-Columbian Mexican Miniatures: The Josef and Anni Albers Collection*, p. 2.

24. Fesci, interview with Albers, July 5, 1968, p. 3.

25. Mary Jane Jacob described the side portions of these two weavings as "margin-like borders." Jacob, "Anni Albers: A Modern Weaver as Artist," p. 93.

26. Polsky, interview with Albers, Jan. 11, 1985, p. 43.

27. Welliver, "A Conversation with Anni Albers," p. 22. Albers frequently referred to her pictorial work as a *method* of working, as a way for her to approach art and to possibly rise to the level of art. Albers, "Work with Materials" (1937), in Albers, *On Designing* (Middletown, Conn.: Wesleyan University Press, 1971, 1987), p. 52.

28. Albers, introduction, in *Anni Albers: Pictorial Weavings* (exh. cat.; Cambridge, Mass.: MIT Press, 1959), p. 3.

29. Rebecca Stone-Miller, *Art of the Andes from Chavin to Inca* (London: Thames and Hudson, 1995), p. 212.

30. Polsky, interview with Albers, Jan. 11, 1985, pp. 45–46.

31. Albers, *On Weaving*, p. 68.

32. For this technique, the cloth was woven with a short vertical warp and long, pattern-carrying weft threads in the horizontal direction. Thus the Andean weaver was oriented "sideways" to the final design, a feat that required great mental and visual dexterity. See Stone-Miller, *To Weave for the Sun*, p. 38.

33. Klee's *Carpet of Memory* (*Teppich der Erinnerung*, 1914), for example, was originally made in a vertical direction and then turned horizontally. Susanna Partsch, *Paul Klee* (Cologne: Benedikt Taschen, 1993), p. 28.

34. In the same year that Albers wove *Two* the first major De Stijl exhibition was presented at the Museum of Modern Art in New York. It is likely that Albers saw the exhibition, because at the time she was visiting New York regularly to conduct research with the Andean textile scholar Junius B. Bird at the American Museum of Natural History. Correspondence between Junius B. Bird and Anni Albers, February and March 1952, Junius B. Bird Papers, American Museum of Natural History, New York.
Albers wrote at least one scholarly article on the subject of Andean weaving techniques, "A Structural Process in Weaving," written in 1952 for a course she attended at Yale University, which was taught by George Kubler. Albers revised the essay after a lengthy correspondence with Bird, and it was subsequently published in *On Designing*. In it, Albers investigated how Andean weavers were able to weave large widths of cloth on hand looms, concluding that the weavers must have utilized a triple- or quadruple-layer technique on frame looms; each plane of warps must have been woven accordion-style so that, when unfolded, it yielded a single web of greater dimensions than the loom itself. Susan Niles, in her article "Artist and Empire in Inca Colonial Textiles," in Stone-Miller, *To Weave for the Sun*, p. 56, proposed that the weavers used a hinged loom, which would also have produced a large web. Considering that Albers was not a textile scholar per se, her solution to this problem was advanced for the time.

35. It is likely that Albers was familiar with the journal *De Stijl* from her Bauhaus years. In addition, she and Josef owned *Principles of Neo-Plastic Art*, edited by Theo van Doesburg and published by the Bauhaus in 1925. Albers is said to have liked van Doesburg's work, and may have met him in Germany before his death in 1932. Conversation with Nicholas Fox Weber, Nov. 18, 1966.

36. See Rebecca Stone-Miller, "Camelids and Chaos in Huari and Tiwanaku Textiles," in Richard Townsend, ed., *The Ancient Americas* (exh. cat.; Chicago: Art Institute of Chicago, 1992), p. 336, for a discussion of Andean abstraction. For a summary of De Stijl, see Yve-Alain Bois, "The De Stijl Idea," in *Painting as Model* (Cambridge, Mass.: MIT Press, 1990).

37. A large Klee memorial exhibition was held at the Museum of Modern Art in 1941. The accompanying catalogue, *Paul Klee*, edited by Margaret Miller, was revised and expanded in 1945. Albers had easy access to numerous exhibitions of Klee's work in galleries and museums in New York. For example, sixty works by Klee were exhibited at the Buchholz Gallery from January to February 1951, and thirty-one works were exhibited at the New Art Circle from April to May 1952.

38. A pictograph is a sign with figurative references, as Albers used in *Monte Alban*. In titling *Pictographic*, however, she used the term in a more general way, as the work does not refer to an external figurative subject but rather to the notion and the image of mark-making.

39. Fleischmann describes this purchase in her travel diaries, p. 24.

40. Albers, "Handweaving Today—Textile Work at Black Mountain College," *The Weaver* 6, no. 1 (Jan.–Feb. 1941), p. 3.

41. Albers, *On Weaving*, p. 69.

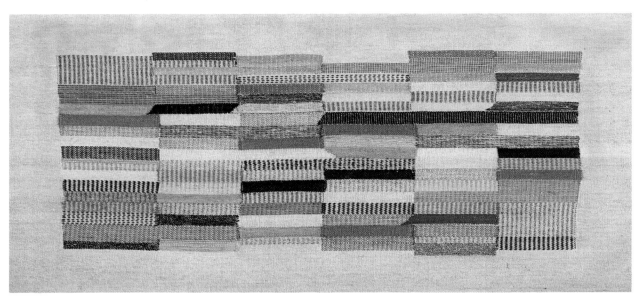

36. *Untitled*, 1934.
Rayon, linen, cotton, wool, and jute,
53.3 × 116.8 cm (21 × 46 inches).
Collection of Mrs. John Wilkie,
New York.

37. *Ancient Writing*, 1936.
Rayon, linen, cotton, and jute,
149.8 × 111 cm (59 × 43 11/16 inches).
National Museum of American Art,
Smithsonian Institution,
Washington, D.C.,
Gift of John Young 1984.150.

38. *Monte Alban*, 1936. Silk, linen, and wool,
146 × 112 cm (57 ⅜ × 44 inches).
The Busch-Reisinger Museum,
Harvard University Art Museums,
Cambridge, Massachusetts,
Gift of Mr. and Mrs. Richard G. Leahy
BR 81.5.

39. *La Luz I*, 1947.
Cotton, hemp, and metallic gimp,
47 × 82.5 cm (18 ½ × 32 ½ inches).
The Josef and Anni Albers Foundation,
Bethany.

40. *Untitled*, 1948. Linen and cotton,
41.9 × 49.5 cm (16½ × 19½ inches).
The Museum of Modern Art,
New York, Edgar Kaufmann, Jr. Fund
200.50.

41. *Cityscape*, 1949. Bast and cotton,
44.5 × 67.3 cm (17 ½ × 26 ½ inches).
Collection of Ruth Agoos Villalovos.

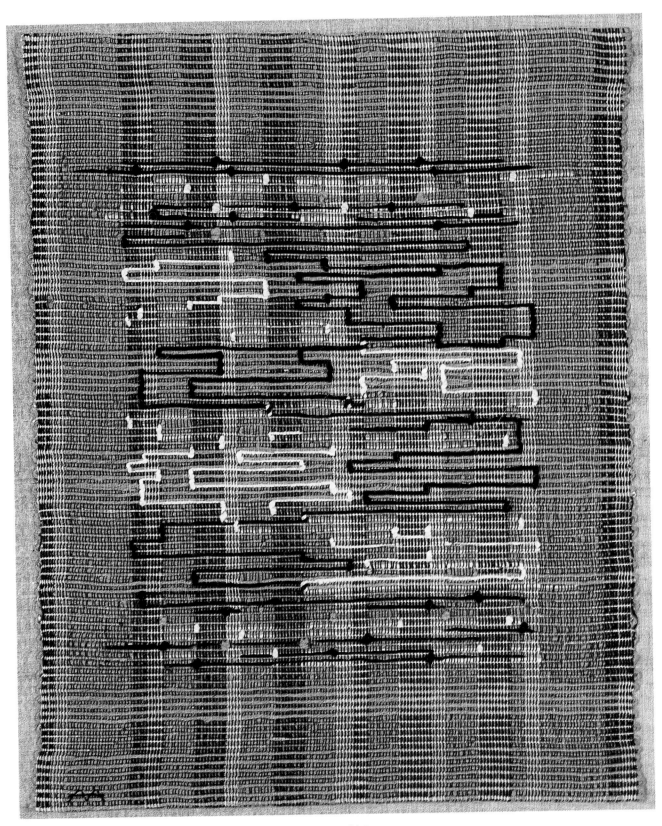

42. *Black-White-Gold I*, 1950.
Cotton, jute, and metallic ribbon,
63.5 × 48.3 cm (25 × 19 inches).
The Josef and Anni Albers Foundation,
Bethany.

43. *Development in Rose I*, 1952.
Cotton and hemp,
57 × 43.8 cm (22 ⁷⁄₁₆ × 17 ¼ inches).
The Josef and Anni Albers Foundation,
Bethany.

44. *Two,* 1952. Linen, cotton, and rayon,
46.4 × 104 cm (18¼ × 41 inches).
The Josef and Anni Albers Foundation,
Bethany, Gift of John Norton and
Lucia N. Woodruff.

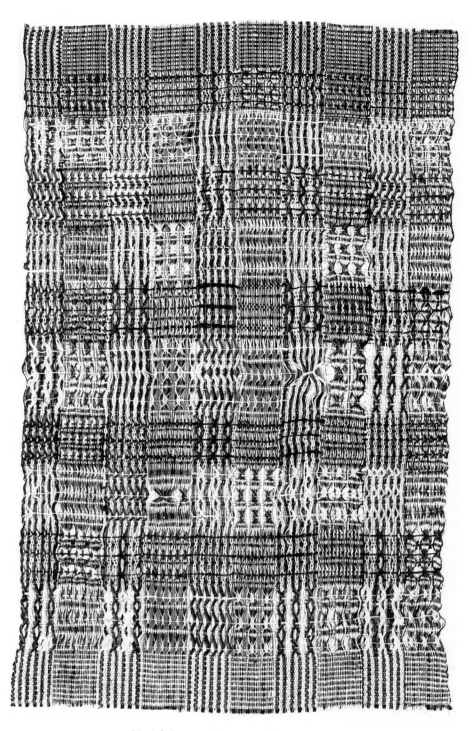

45. *Untitled*, 1950. Cotton and bast,
64.8 × 38.1 cm (25 ½ × 15 inches).
Cunningham Dance Foundation,
New York.

46. *Red Meander*, 1954. Linen and
cotton, 65 × 50 cm (25 ⅛ × 19 ¹¹⁄₁₆ inches).
Collection of Ruth Agoos Villalovos.

47. *Play of Squares*, 1955.
Wool and linen,
87.6 × 62.2 cm (34½ × 24½ inches).
The Currier Gallery of Art,
Manchester, New Hampshire,
Currier Funds 1956.3.

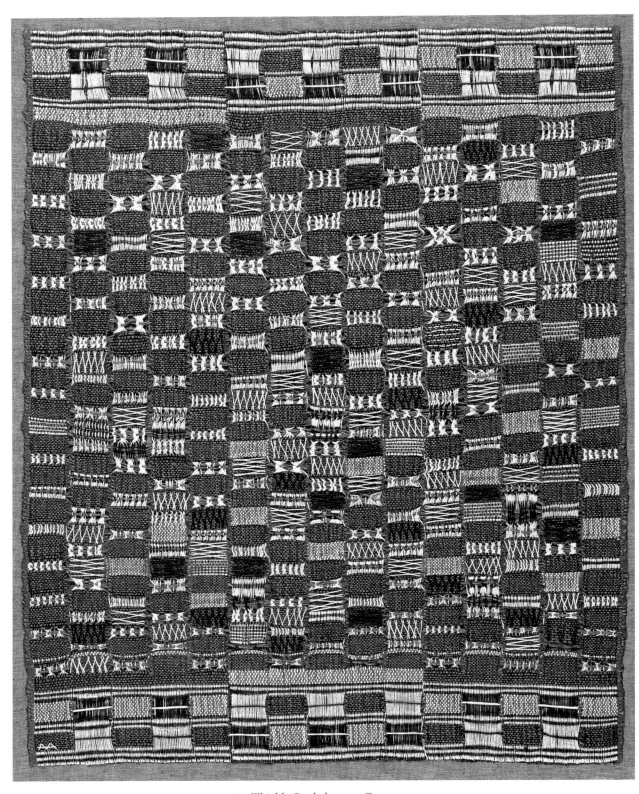

48. *Thickly Settled*, 1957. Cotton
and jute, 78.7 × 62 cm (31 × 24⅛ inches).
Yale University Art Gallery,
New Haven, Connecticut,
Director's Purchase Fund 1972.83.

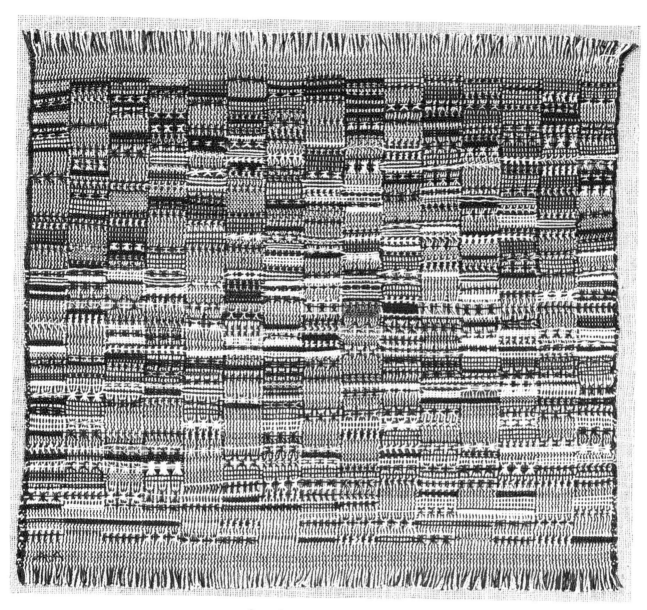

49. *Open Letter*, 1958. Cotton,
58.4 × 59.7 cm (23 × 23 ½ inches).
The Josef and Anni Albers Foundation,
Bethany.

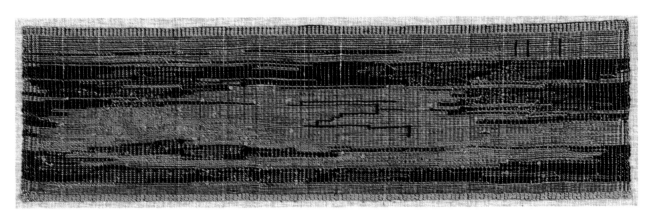

50. *In the Landscape*, 1958.
Cotton and jute,
29.5 × 98.5 cm (11 ⅛ × 38 ¹³⁄₁₆ inches).
Collection of Dr. William and
Constance G. Kantar.

51. *South of the Border*, 1958.
Cotton and wool,
10.6 × 38.7 cm (4 ³⁄₁₆ × 15 ³⁄₁₆ inches).
The Baltimore Museum of Art,
Decorative Arts and Contemporary
Crafts Fund 1959.91.

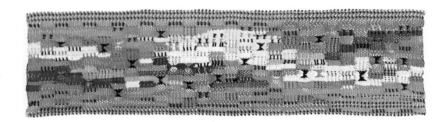

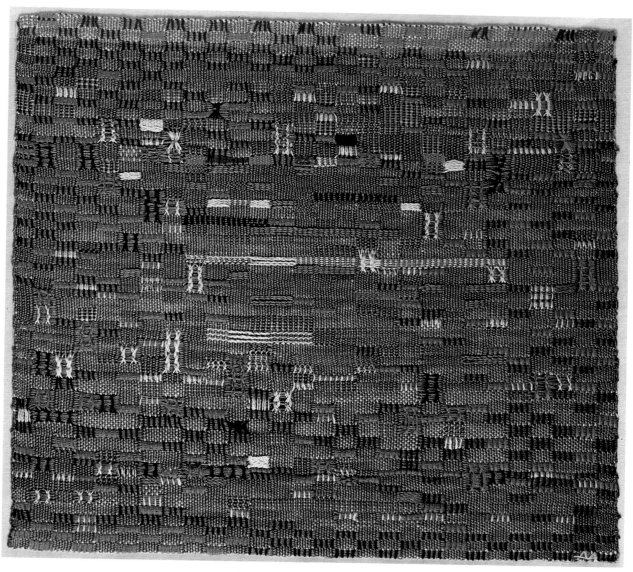

52. *Pasture*, 1958. Mercerized cotton,
35.6 × 39.4 cm (14 1/16 × 15 1/2 inches).
The Metropolitan Museum of Art,
New York, Purchase, Edward C.
Moore, Jr., Gift, 1969 69.135.

53. *Red and Blue Layers*, 1954. Cotton,
61 × 36.8 cm (24 × 14½ inches).
The Josef and Anni Albers Foundation,
Bethany, Formerly collection of
Mrs. Eleanor Grossman.

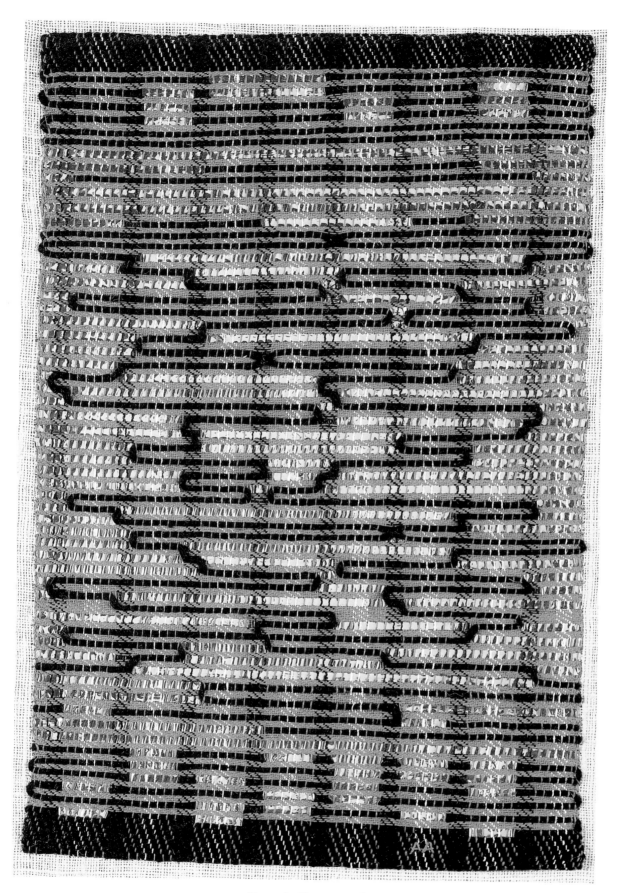

54. *From the East*, 1963. Cotton and plastic,
65.4 × 42 cm (25 × 16½ inches).
The Josef and Anni Albers Foundation,
Bethany.

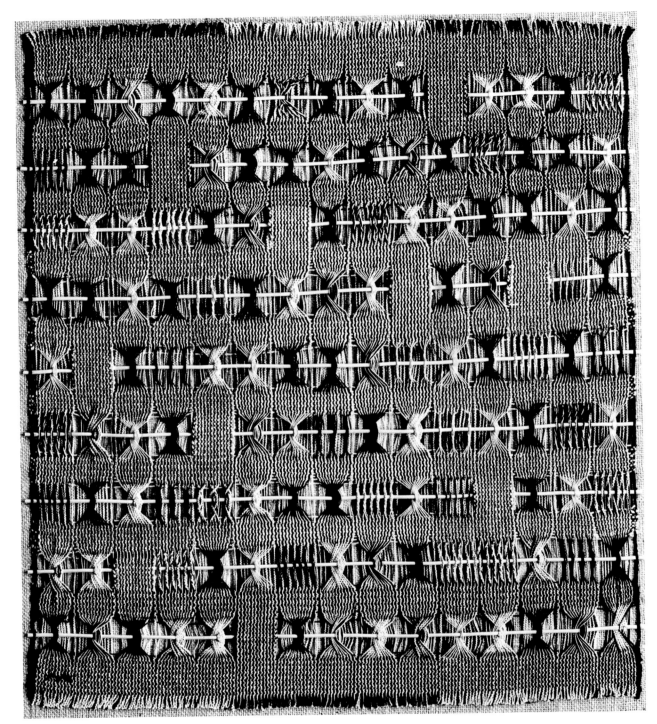

55. *Variation on a Theme*, 1958.
Cotton, linen, and plastic,
87.6 × 77.5 cm (34½ × 30½inches).
Collection of Dr. and Mrs.
Theodore Dreier, Jr.

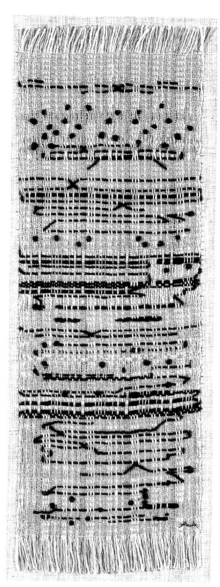

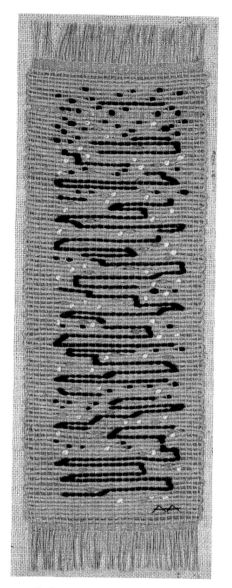

56. *Haiku,* 1961. Cotton, hemp,
and metallic thread,
57.2 × 18.4 cm (22½ × 7¼ inches).
The Josef and Anni Albers Foundation,
Bethany.

57. *Code,* 1962. Cotton, hemp,
and metallic thread,
58.4 × 18.4 cm (23 × 7¼ inches).
The Josef and Anni Albers Foundation,
Bethany.

58. *Intersecting*, 1962.
Cotton and rayon, 40 × 42 cm
(15 ¹¹⁄₁₆ × 16 ½ inches).
Collection of Katharine and
Nicholas Weber.

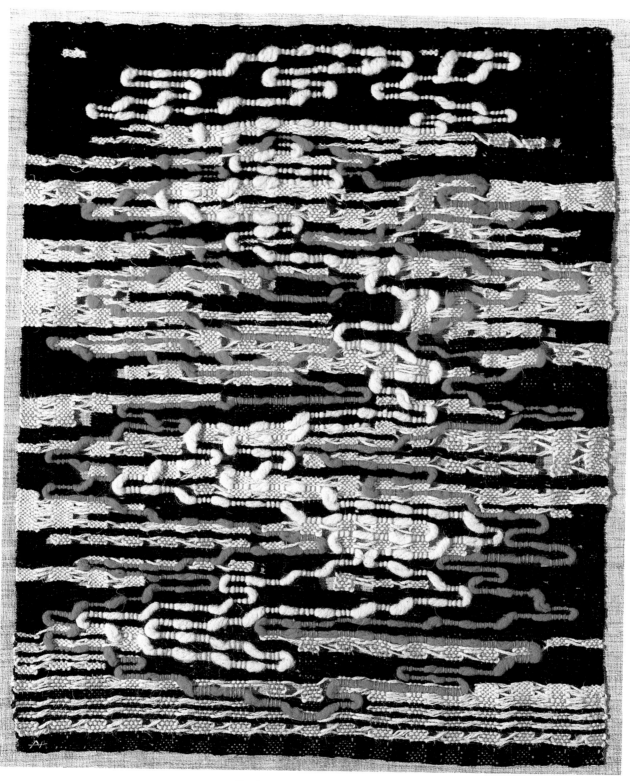

59. *Under Way*, 1963.
Cotton, linen, and wool,
74 × 61.2 cm (29 ⅛ × 24 ⅛ inches).
Hirshhorn Museum and
Sculpture Garden, Smithsonian
Institution, Washington, D.C.,
Bequest of Joseph H. Hirshhorn,
1986.

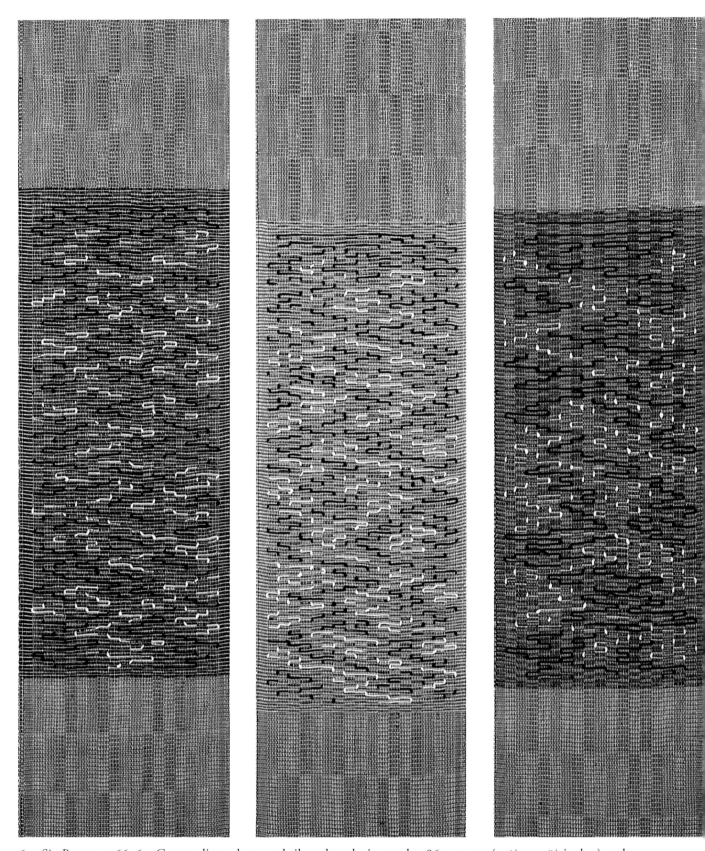

60. *Six Prayers*, 1966–67. Cotton, linen, bast, and silver thread; six panels, 186 × 50 cm (73 ⅛ × 19 ¹¹⁄₁₆ inches) each. The Jewish Museum, New York, Gift of Albert A. List Family JM149-71-6.

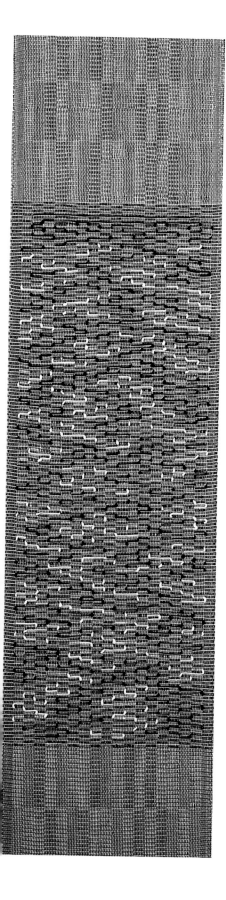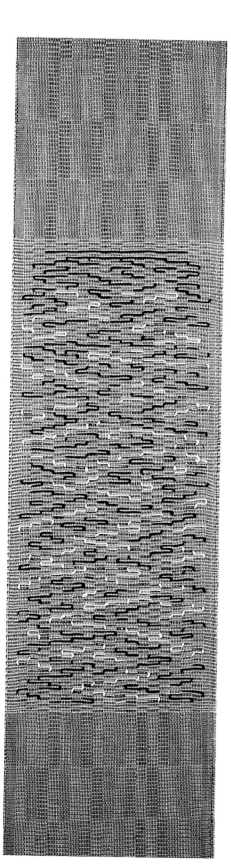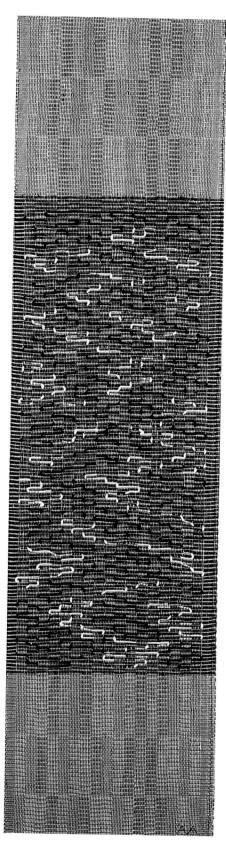

On the Structure of the Weavings
Jean-Paul Leclercq

61. Detail of *Two*, 1952 (see cat. no. 44).

Two (1952) presents a strictly orthogonal pattern in dark brown and yellow. There are several right-angle direction changes, but the entire pattern is organized around the basic unit of the square. The plain-weave checkerboard ground in subtly contrasting tones gives the piece its rhythm. The result is very different from the hangings that Albers made at the Bauhaus; the patterns of those works are also strictly orthogonal, but are built on intersecting rectilinear strips of unequal width.

In works with abstract patterns, the direction in which the piece should be viewed is difficult to determine if one does not understand the designer's intentions. In *Two*, Albers indicated the direction by adding her embroidered signature at the lower right. The warp in this work is horizontal, not vertical; the piece was woven lengthwise, in the direction of the warp, but has a transversal pattern, to be read weftwise. Although generally uncommon, examples of textiles with a pattern in the weft direction can be found in the European tradition, such as the mid-fifteenth-century altar-front pieces comprised of a single width of figured gold brocaded velvet used horizontally, with a very large pattern unit made of a single comber unit. Patterns in the weft direction are also found in late-eighteenth-century textiles in which the pattern has a top end intended for furniture borders; these are woven in two or more bands within the width of the fabric. In such cases, the width of the fabric becomes the height of the pattern, and the pattern width is thus independent of the fabric's width.

The pattern in *Two* is formed by an additional twill float, and the thick white weft—that is, every other ground pick—therefore floats to the back, without binding.

The checkerboard ground perfectly illustrates Albers's interest in texture, material, and structure. While the weave does not change, variations in appearance are achieved through the warping, the shuttling order, and the binary properties of the plain weave. The warping alternates between a thick dark cream thread and a thinner white thread. During the weaving, Albers alternately passed a thin black weft pick and then a thick white weft pick, thus creating the two different combinations.

In the dark squares, the thick dark cream warp binds and covers the thick white weft, and, conversely, the fine black weft can easily be seen because it goes to the front above the thick warp. This is what produces dominant lines in the direction of the weft that alternate between black and dark cream. In the light squares, the thick white weft is bound only by the thin white warp, but it is set apart when it is above the thick dark cream warp, which binds the fine black weft on the front, keeping it rather hidden.

The checkerboard pattern is created very simply, by inverting evenness at the end of each square. In the direction of the weft, going from one square to another is accomplished by warping two consecutive threads from the same warp; in the direction of the warp, it is executed during weaving, with two consecutive picks of the same weft.

The possibilities afforded by the play of even and odd (or alternating) threads are very important in plain weave and its variations (like the addition of weft or warp cords), and the fact that Albers drew on these possibilities here reflects her tendency to play with structure and material. But she would have found an identical example among the samples included in a study conducted around 1790 of fabrics manufactured in France.[1] In this eighteenth-century example, the threads are finer and there is no pattern other than the one produced by the plain weave and the warp and weft materials. Yet the evenness inversions are made with two dark blue threads, or two dark blue picks, while the other threads, in both the weft and the warp, alternate between white and pale blue. Thus the squares have a dark outline and the checkerboard resembles a tabby on the scale of basketwork made of large twigs. Blue and white lines are created by the material and the weave; in one square (which resembles a vertical rectangle), they follow the direction of the warp, while in the next (which resembles a horizontal rectangle), they follow the direction of the weft. The result is a fabric that appears to consist of weft and warp threads as wide as these squares and bound in the form of a plain weave.

1. Registre d'Enquête Industrielle, *Toiles et Toileries* (Paris, ca. 1790), Musée de la Mode et du Textile, Palais du Louvre, Paris, Union Centrale des Arts Décoratifs, p. 329.

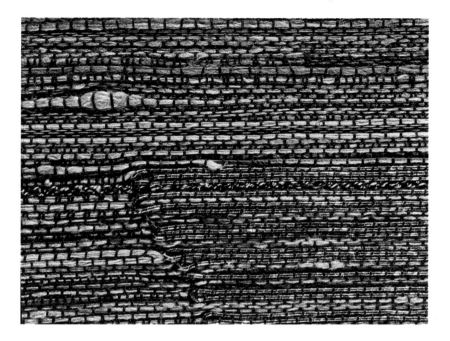

62. Detail of *La Luz I*, 1947 (see cat. no. 39).

At first, *La Luz I* (1947) seems to have a graphic quality that is foreign to the rest of Albers's work and to the Bauhaus aesthetic: its symmetrical pattern suggests a cross or some sort of symbolic bird, such as an eagle. The piece's scale, however, allows us to perceive the individual play of threads, with twelve warp threads and seven weft picks per centimeter. The latter number varies greatly, as the thick brownish-yellow weft is approximately half a centimeter wide. Some of the processes used by Albers in this work can be found later in her calligraphic-style "pictorial weavings."

This is a short, horizontal piece, wider in the weft direction than it is long in the warp direction. The basic weave, as it appears at the top and bottom in the plain strips, comes from the warp twill (3/1, S direction), with the space between warp threads giving the textile a dominant weft. But elsewhere it varies, very irregularly in the ground, and there are also additional brocading wefts. In some places these brocading wefts are bound in plain weave by several consecutive warp threads, while the other warp threads float freely to the back, thus introducing a local binding system between two ground picks. These are the kinds of liberties allowed by tapestry work as it was practiced by the Copts. The

brocading is not on top of the binding system, but rather introduces its own system, using the same warp threads as the ground weave on several consecutive picks.

Despite the general simplicity of the pattern, Albers played with both the material and the weave; the ground's varied shuttling order competes with the integration of the brocading and with area weave variations to remove any seeming repetitions. Irregularities are created through weaving by the inclusion of additional wefts in certain areas, and elsewhere they are obtained through material, by the use of complex or uneven thread.

In the main pattern, the brocaded thread repeatedly returns on the front, rather than on the back, to get to its next starting point. Technically facilitated by weaving on the front, this Andean process, which is still practiced today, is used in all of Albers's "pictorial weavings." The process accentuates the continuity of the weft thread from one pick to the next, exposing its vertical course as well as its horizontal one. This produces rounded shapes, oblique lines—which, in other pieces by Albers, such as *From the East* (1963), are sometimes crossed—or even vertical lines (in which case the weft thread runs parallel to the warp thread). For these shapes and lines to be visible, the scale of the weft thread in relation to the pattern and to the textile has to be large enough for the course of a single thread to be seen, as it is in Albers's *Black-White-Gold I* (1950), *Haiku* (1961), *Code* (1962), *Intersecting* (1962), and *From the East*.

The technique of placing the returns of the brocading thread on the front was

used in fifteenth-century velvets with gold-thread brocaded elements for technical reasons, but in these works it seems to have been a constraint, rather than an element of the pattern; the patterns are figurative and the gold filé is much too fine for its graphic quality to have been utilized. In other European examples, these returns appear more often on the backs of the textiles, or along the selvages, where the pattern weft thread does not integrate into the selvage weave. In such works, the continuity of the weft thread from one pick to the next is a hidden feature and does not have a prominent graphic quality, which is a violation of a fundamental premise of Western textiles.

63. Detail of *In the Landscape*, 1958
(see cat. no. 50).

In the Landscape (1958), like *La Luz I* (1947), is also a horizontal piece with a short warp. It has a striped and banded plain weave, with brocading that shifts about on the face and is vertical in certain areas.

With warping that alternates between fine black threads and thick threads in various colors, the textile, which is loosely woven, presents a dominant weft, though its weave appears to have a square pattern because the warp threads bind the weft picks of the same material. Like the warping, the shuttling order alternates between a fine black weft and a thick colored weft, except in the bands at the top and bottom, where a thick orange-yellow thread is used exclusively in the weft.

Elsewhere, the black warp (the odd thread) binds the black weft (the odd pick), and as both are fine they are rather inconspicuous. Meanwhile, the colored warp (the even thread) binds the colored weft (the even pick), both of which have heavy sections. In some areas, the basic

lat changes color according to a tapestry technique, but it is still bound by the colored warp.

The brocading pick is added on the front of the binding system, which is tabby. The black warp threads bind the brocading lat with the fine black weft simultaneously, with the two passes together in the shed. When it is bound by the fine black warp in this way, the brocading pick, which is dark blue, is barely interrupted visually and appears to be continuous, winding above the squarelike ground produced by the plain weave.

This is a good example of the diverse uses of a single weave, which here has been varied through the unique possibilities offered by the warping, the shuttling order, and the local doubling of one of the two ground picks with a brocading pick. This produces a double tabby weave, which is typical of silk textiles.

64. Detail of *Black-White-Gold I*, 1950
(see cat. no. 42).

Black-White-Gold I (1950) is a superb
example of Albers's calligraphic-style "pictorial weavings." Like her *La Luz I* (1947)
and *In the Landscape* (1958), it is also presented in the direction of the warp, but it
is longer in the direction of the warp than
it is in the direction of the weft—that is,
its larger dimension is not horizontal.
Here again Albers used a striped, banded,
and brocaded plain weave, playing with the
warping and shuttling order in complex
ways to create a background with squares.

The low density of the weave compared to the scale of the piece—eight warp
threads and three to four weft picks per
centimeter—allows the threads to be read
individually, while the curves of the black
and white brocading picks are highlighted.
The ground weave is patterned in vertical
strips of a single color or a combination
of two colors—black, black and white,
brown and black, or brown—with the

variation in the order: brown jute pick
in the first shed, gold lamella pick in the
second.

The warping alternates between white
odd threads and black even threads, but
because some are thin and others thick,
the visibility of the white and black in the
warp varies. Similarly, the warp reveals
the two alternating wefts, brown jute and
gold lamella, to varying degrees. As a
result, there are four combinations, which
are based on the section of the warp
threads: even and odd threads, all of which
have a heavy section; even and odd threads,
all of which have a delicate section; only
odd threads with a heavy section; only even
threads with a heavy section. The lamella
and the jute are bound is some places by
the white odd threads, and in other places
by the black even threads. The luster of the
lamella is interrupted most emphatically
when the warp binding it is black and wide.

The inversion in this piece is vertical,
created by two consecutive jute picks,
following the principle of evenness inversions. (Albers's *Two* [1952] is an example
of double evenness inversion, in both the
warp and the weft.)

65. Detail of *Intersecting*, 1962
(see cat. no. 58).

Intersecting (1962), a striped, banded, and
brocaded tabby, presents a particularly
distinct use of the curves of brocading on
the face. The white, orange, and blue
brocaded thread contrasts in some cases
with the warp thread and ground lat but
not in others, yielding several inversions
of contrast and readability. Generally, the
brocaded threads are bound by the same
warp threads, as there is a proportion of
one brocading pick for every two ground
picks; it is tabby bound, however, where
there is one brocading pick for every
ground pick.

66. Detail of *From the East*, 1963
(see cat. no. 54).

From the East (1963) transforms the common look of a warp twill 3/1 using only its shuttling order. The pass has one more pick than the weave: a wide gold lamella, which is followed by four picks of a fine orange weft. This produces a gold lamella binding in warp twill 3/1, resembling a binding by the same warp threads on all picks.

Here Albers was not playing with even and odd: the warp is prepared with eight repetitions of a sequence comprised of eight black threads, eight orange threads, eight white threads, and eight more orange threads. The degree to which the luster of the lamella is interrupted by the bindings depends on the color of the ends. As is often the case with Albers's "pictorial weavings," one has to search for the ground weave (from which variations have been made) in the bands that start and end the textile, which in this work have an all-black weft.

Being supple, the lamella sinks below the bindings, losing its flatness and taking on an appearance similar to the pleated lamellas used by embroiderers in the seventeenth and eighteenth centuries. This resemblance, which most likely is fortuitous, can be found in many of Albers's works, as well as in examples from Europe's textile tradition.

More interesting is Albers's violation of the usual distinction between the ground pick, the *liseré* lat, and the brocading lat. The lamella comprises part of the twill ground weave, like each of the orange weft picks, but seems to have an effect like a *liseré* lat. This results from its width, which is greater than that of the orange band formed by the four orange weft picks that follow. Conversely, like a brocading lat, the lamella stops where the thick black weft passes; this weft then replaces the lamella in the warp twill 3/1 weave that is formed with the orange weft, but it continues in a winding fashion, like a brocading pick, on the face (in accordance with Albers's favorite principle), and returns to the place where it will next replace the lamella. The relief has been enhanced by the use of the beater in places where the lamella is almost absent in a single pick. The higher relief is met in two areas, where two of the black threads cross in an *X.* Here two or more small hand shuttles have been used for a single medium, another characteristic of brocading; only one shuttle is used for a single material when it involves a ground lat, a *liseré* lat, or a weft-patterning lat, since the passage is performed with a shuttle across the entire width of the fabric.

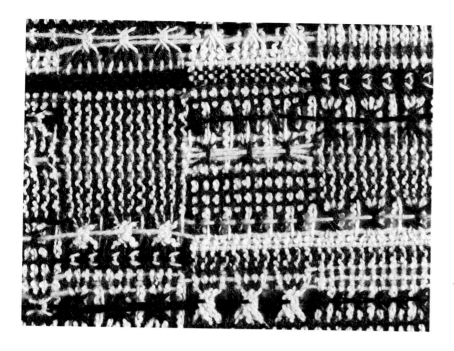

67. Detail of *Open Letter*, 1958
(see cat. no. 49).

Open Letter (1958) is based on a plain weave, with gauze variations in several areas. It is a prime example of Albers's use of the binary as an organizing principle in her weaving.

The warping is composed of a sequence of two white threads (the first of which is a spiral thread) followed by two black threads; hence the warping unit consists of four threads, with the first two in a different and contrasting material than that of the last two. As a result, the work has a two-level, binary aspect.

There are twelve warping units, or forty-eight warp threads altogether, and the weaving effects are organized in strips of equal width that follow the direction of the warp. These strips are divided horizontally at intervals by bands of plain weave that traverse the width of the fabric; even though these bands are practically imperceptible, they produce a pattern of squares. The red from the brocading pick is added in places to the black and white of the warp and the ground weft. In plain-weave areas involving all the threads, the spiral thread—its winding quality highlighted by the two black threads of the warping unit—lends a dense gauze look to the fabric, which is due not to the texture of the fabric, but rather to the composite nature of the thread. Although Albers used threads with irregular sections in this and other pieces, she preferred to play with weaves; for her, textile art lay in the weave, rather than in the effect of the threads.

Elsewhere, the plain weave brings out the color contrast between the warp threads: the white areas are woven with white weft threads that are bound only by the white warp threads, the two black threads of the warping unit floating to the back; the black areas, on the other hand, are woven with black weft threads that are bound only by the black warp threads, the two white threads of the warping unit floating to the back.

In the areas where there are black rectangles on a white background, the weave becomes an extended tabby with two warp threads; the white weft is bound, in alternating fashion, by the two black warp threads and the two white ones. The principle is the same in the areas with white rectangles on a black background, but here the weft is black instead of white.

In the areas with black ribs striped with white, the weft is black and the binding alternates between the two black warp threads and the second, thin white warp thread; the white spiral warp thread floats to the back. The warp tension causes the two ribs corresponding to the black weft binding to protrude, by a single warp thread, which is white. The relief inverts with the following weft pick, which is bound on the face with the two black threads; the same principle, but in reverse, applies also to the white weft.

The many gauze effects in the piece are produced by various combinations of the different weft and warp thread types, textures, and colors. The black and white warp and weft threads that are not used act as a visual base for the deviating warp threads that serve as the gauze. The visual effect is thus better controlled than with a transparent gauze that involves all the threads and picks, as in this case the effect is uncertain since it depends on the surface under the piece. Instances of the gauze technique used by Albers in this work can be found in the European textile tradition; among the gauzes by Tabourier, Bisson et Cie that were presented at the 1889 World Fair, for example, was a two-color piece, with green weft and warp gauze on a pink background and unused weft threads floating without binding to the back.

In specific areas, there is both a red brocaded weft and an additional weft in either white or black that is woven in a tabby with one of the warps. Here the visual distinction between ground pick and brocading pick is blurred.

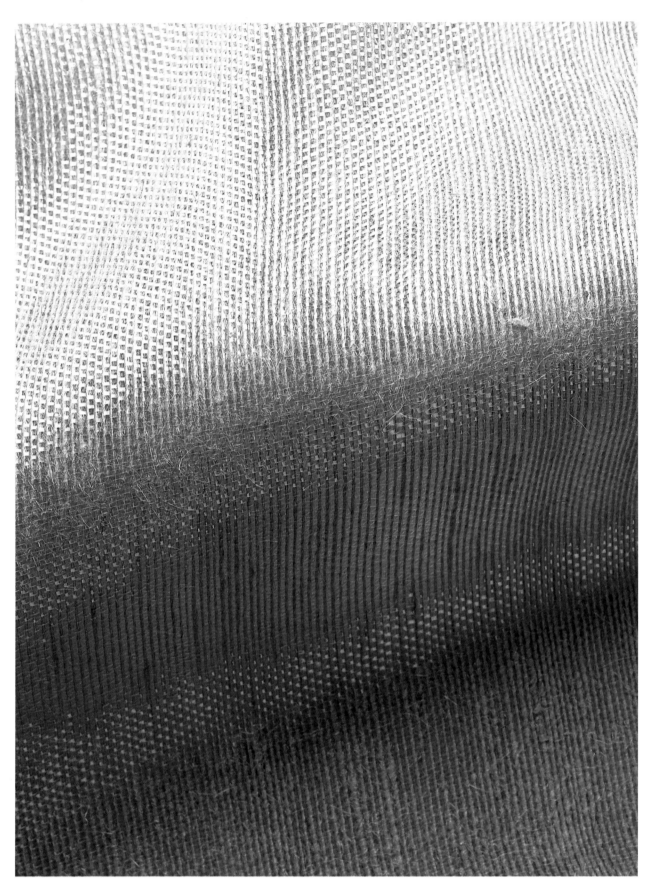

68. Textile sample, ca. 1945.
Cellophane and jute, 91 × 101.5 cm
(35 ⅞ × 40 inches). The Metropolitan
Museum of Art, New York,
Gift of Anni Albers 1970.75.9.

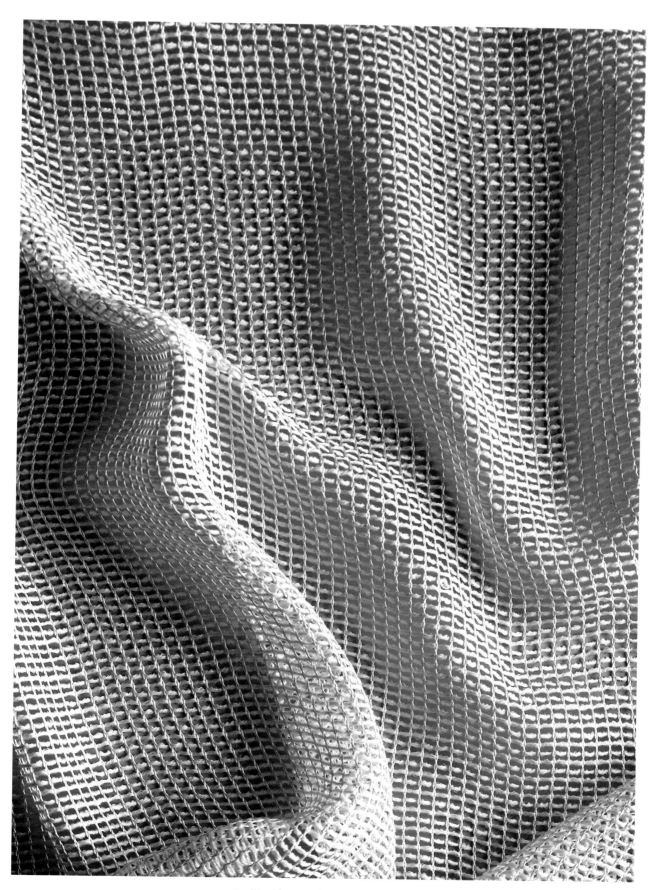

69. Textile sample, ca. 1960. Linen,
90 × 133 cm (35⅛ × 52⅜ inches).
The Metropolitan Museum of Art,
New York, Gift of Anni Albers
1970.75.16.

70. Drapery material, ca. 1935.
Cellophane, rayon, and cotton,
320 × 82.5 cm (126 × 32 ½ inches).
The Museum of Modern Art,
New York, Gift of the designer
67.75.SC.

71. Drapery material, 1961.
Jute and metallic thread,
121.9 × 132.1 cm (48 × 52 inches).
The Museum of Modern Art,
New York, Gift of the designer
68.75.SC.

72. Drapery material, ca. 1948.
Cotton and metallic thread,
174 × 109.2 cm (68 ½ × 43 inches).
The Museum of Modern Art,
New York, Gift of the designer
63.75.SC.

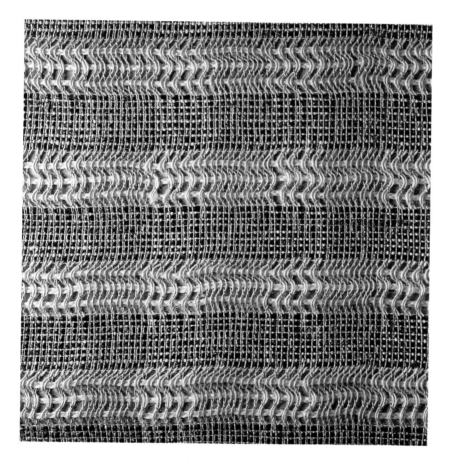

73. Partition material, ca. 1949.
Cotton, jute, horsehair,
and cellophane, 151 × 85 cm
(59 ⅜ × 33 ½ inches).
The Metropolitan Museum of Art,
New York, Gift of Anni Albers
1970.75.12.

74. Wall-covering material,
ca. 1930. Linen and cellophane,
325.1 × 119.4 cm (128 × 47 inches).
The Metropolitan Museum of Art,
New York, Gift of Anni Albers
1970.75.4.

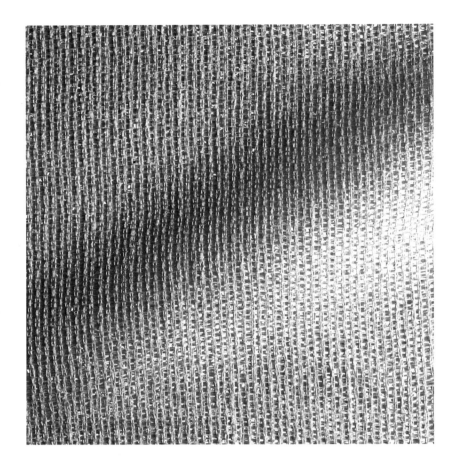

75. Textile sample, ca. 1935.
Cellophane, cotton, and rayon,
174 × 82 cm (68 ½ × 32 ⅛ inches).
The Metropolitan Museum of Art,
New York, Gift of Anni Albers
1970.75.13.

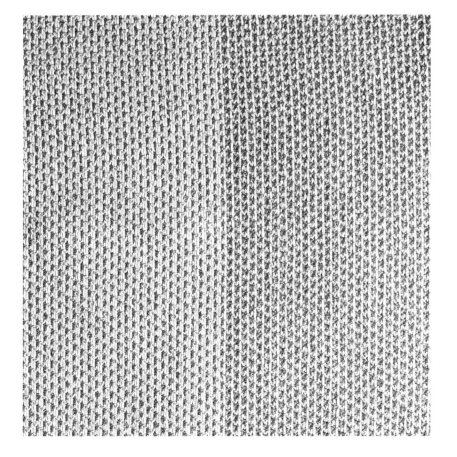

76. Textile sample, 1940. Rayon,
260.4 × 81.3 cm (102½ × 32 inches).
The Metropolitan Museum of Art, New York,
Gift of Anni Albers 1970.75.11.

77. Textile sample, date unknown.
Cotton, 28 × 20 cm
(11 × 7⅞ inches).
The Metropolitan Museum of Art,
New York, Gift of Anni Albers
1970.75.72.

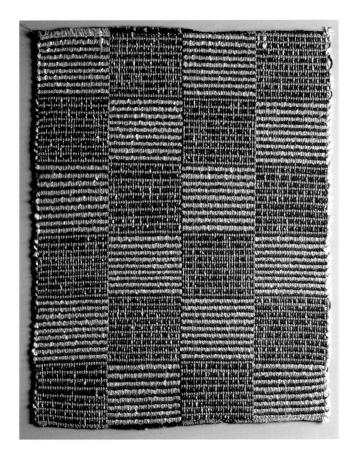

78. Textile sample, date unknown.
Cotton and wool,
28.5 × 20 cm (11¼ × 7⅞ inches).
The Metropolitan Museum of Art,
New York, Gift of Anni Albers
1970.75.69.

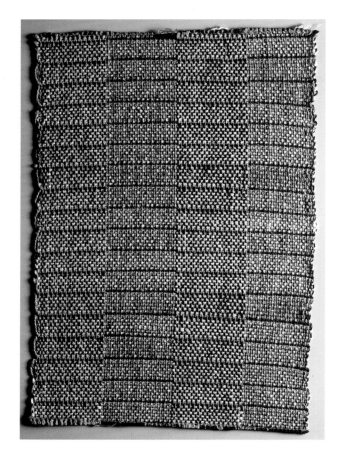

79. Textile sample, date unknown.
Cotton and wool,
28.5 × 19 cm (11¼ × 7½ inches).
The Metropolitan Museum of Art,
New York, Gift of Anni Albers
1970.75.70.

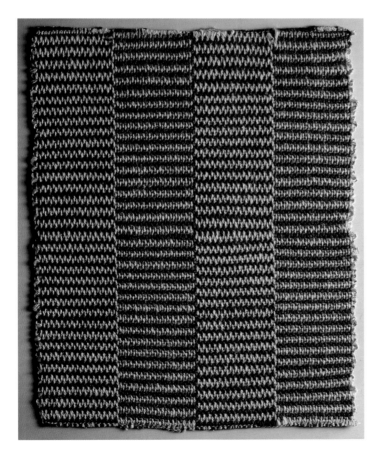

80. Textile sample, date unknown.
Cotton and linen,
27 × 20.5 cm (10⅛ × 8⅛ inches).
The Metropolitan Museum of Art,
New York, Gift of Anni Albers
1970.75.68.

81. Textile sample, date unknown.
Cotton and jute,
28 × 21 cm (11 × 8 ¼ inches).
The Metropolitan Museum of Art,
New York, Gift of Anni Albers
1970.75.73.

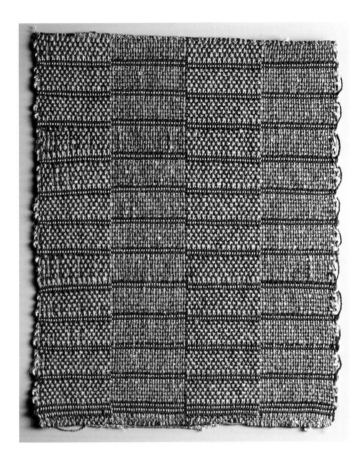

82. Textile sample, date unknown.
Cotton and linen,
28 × 21 cm (11 × 8 ¼ inches).
The Metropolitan Museum of Art,
New York, Gift of Anni Albers
1970.75.71.

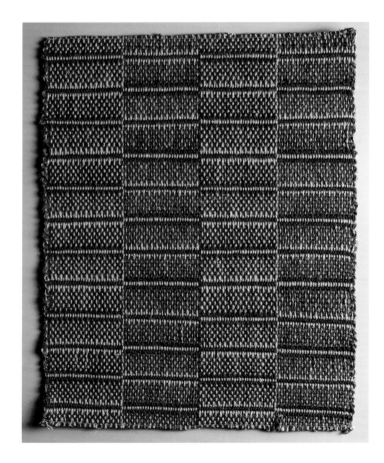

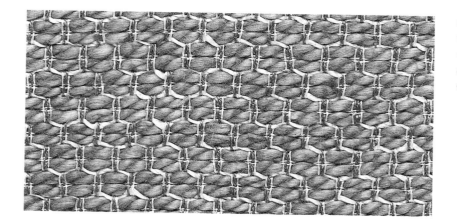

83. Upholstery material, ca. 1929. Cotton and rayon, 11.4 × 19.4 cm (4½ × 7⅝ inches). The Museum of Modern Art, New York, Gift of Josef Albers 450.70.61.

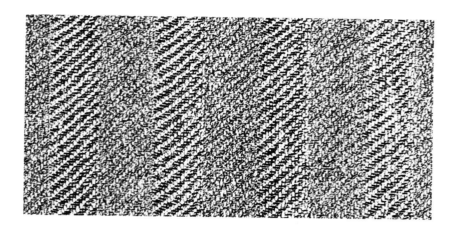

84. Drapery material, date unknown. Cotton and metal foil, 28 × 44 cm (11 × 17⅜ inches). The Metropolitan Museum of Art, New York, Gift of Anni Albers 1970.75.20.

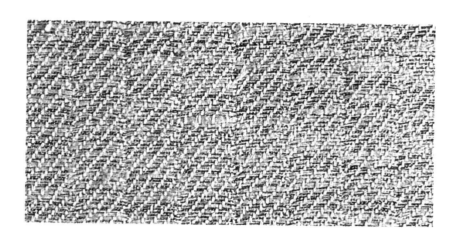

85. Textile sample, ca. 1946. Cotton, linen, and metal foil, 34 × 45 cm (13⅜ × 17¼ inches). The Metropolitan Museum of Art, New York, Gift of Anni Albers 1970.75.18.

86. Wall-covering material, 1929. Raffia, cellophane, and linen, 11.2 × 23.8 cm (4⅜ × 9⅜ inches). The Museum of Modern Art, New York, Gift of the designer 426.51.

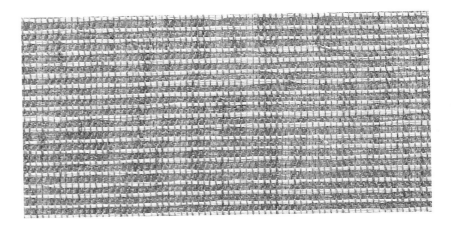

87. Textile sample, probably after 1933. Linen and rayon, 17.7 × 26.6 cm (7 × 10½ inches). The Museum of Modern Art, New York, Gift of Josef Albers 450.70.62.

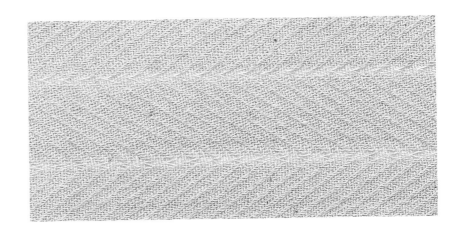

88. Wall-covering material, 1929. Raffia, cellophane, and linen, 11.4 × 30.5 cm (4½ × 12 inches). The Museum of Modern Art, New York, Gift of the designer 424.51.

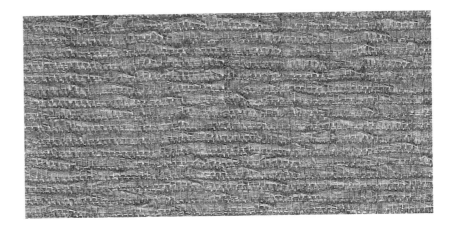

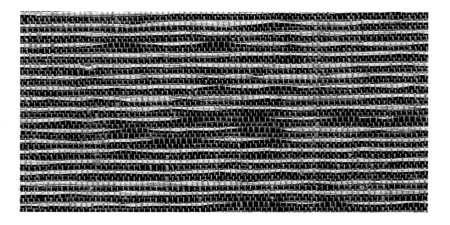

89. Wall-covering material, 1929. Raffia, cellophane, and linen, 11.4 × 30.2 cm (4½ × 11⅞ inches). The Museum of Modern Art, New York, Gift of the designer 421.51.

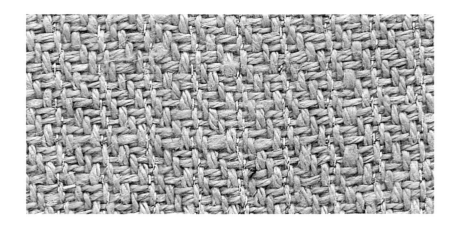

90. Textile sample, probably after 1933. Cotton and rayon, 15.2 × 20.3 cm (6 × 8 inches). The Museum of Modern Art, New York, Gift of Josef Albers 450.70.60.

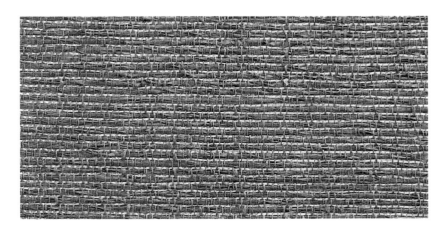

91. Wall-covering material, 1929. Raffia, cellophane, and linen, 11.4 × 30.5 cm (4½ × 12 inches). The Museum of Modern Art, New York, Gift of the designer 423.51.

92. Wall-covering material, probably after 1933. Cellophane, 13.9 × 21 cm (5 ½ × 8 ¼ inches). The Museum of Modern Art, New York, Gift of Josef Albers 450.70.91.

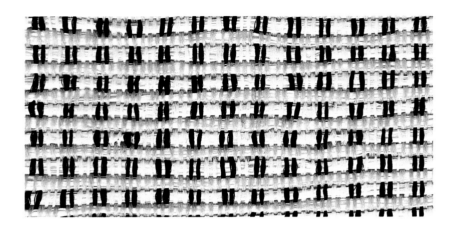

93. Wall-covering material, probably after 1933. Cellophane, 14 × 15.9 cm (5 ½ × 6 ¼ inches). The Museum of Modern Art, New York, Gift of Josef Albers 450.70.93.

94. Wall-covering material, probably after 1933. Cellophane, 12.1 × 15.6 cm (4 ¾ × 6 ⅛ inches). The Museum of Modern Art, New York, Gift of Josef Albers 450.70.92.

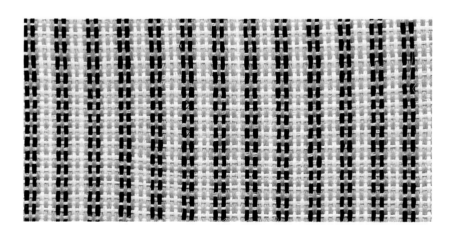

95. Textile sample, ca. 1948.
Fiberglass, 19 × 15 cm
(7 ½ × 5 ⅞ inches).
The Metropolitan Museum of Art,
New York, Gift of Anni Albers
1970.75.59.

96. Textile sample, date unknown.
Cellophane and cotton,
22.5 × 18.5 cm (8 ⅞ × 7 ¼ inches).
The Metropolitan Museum of Art,
New York, Gift of Anni Albers
1970.75.57.

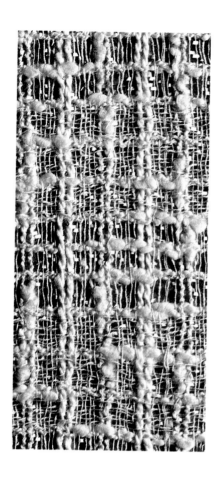

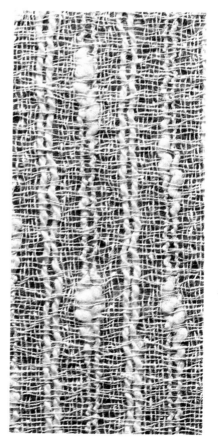

97. Textile sample, date unknown.
Cellophane and cotton,
20 × 19 cm (7 ⅞ × 7 ½ inches).
The Metropolitan Museum of Art,
New York, Gift of Anni Albers
1970.75.56.

98. Textile sample, ca. 1948.
Fiberglass, 21 × 13.5 cm
(8 ¼ × 5 ⅜ inches).
The Metropolitan Museum of Art,
New York, Gift of Anni Albers
1970.75.58.

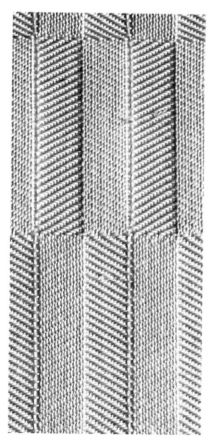

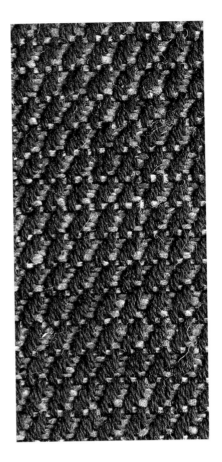

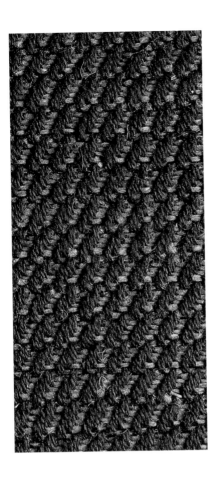

99. Textile sample, date unknown.
Cotton and linen, 28 × 21 cm
(11 × 8 ¼ inches).
The Metropolitan Museum of Art,
New York, Gift of Anni Albers
1970.75.41c.

100. Textile sample, date unknown.
Cotton and linen,
28 × 20.5 cm (11 × 8 ⅛ inches).
The Metropolitan Museum of Art,
New York, Gift of Anni Albers
1970.75.41b.

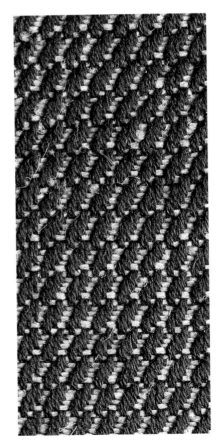

101. Textile sample, date unknown.
Cotton and linen,
27 × 20 cm (10 ⅝ × 7 ⅞ inches).
The Metropolitan Museum of Art,
New York, Gift of Anni Albers
1970.75.41a.

102. Textile sample, date unknown.
Cotton and linen,
27 × 20 cm (10 ⅝ × 7 ⅞ inches).
The Metropolitan Museum of Art,
New York, Gift of Anni Albers
1970.75.43.

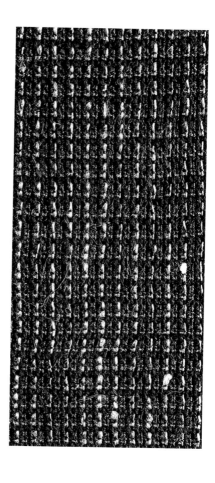

103. Textile sample, date unknown.
Cotton and linen,
23 × 18 cm (9 × 7⅛ inches).
The Metropolitan Museum of Art,
New York, Gift of Anni Albers
1970.75.61.

104. Textile sample, 1950.
Cotton and linen,
26 × 19 cm (10¼ × 7½ inches).
The Metropolitan Museum of Art,
New York, Gift of Anni Albers
1970.75.60.

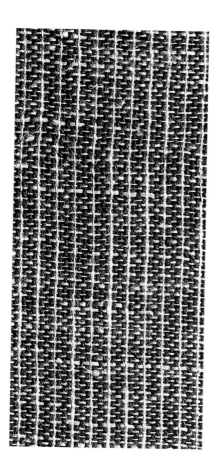

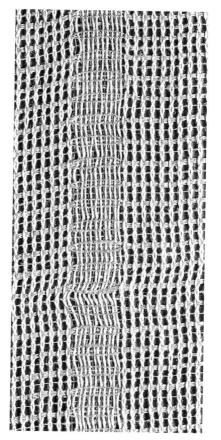

105. Textile sample, ca. 1949.
Linen and metallic thread,
45.5 × 37 cm (17⅞ × 14⅝ inches).
The Metropolitan Museum of Art,
New York, Gift of Anni Albers
1970.75.17.

106. Textile sample, ca. 1959.
Cotton and linen,
42 × 35 cm (16½ × 13¾ inches).
The Metropolitan Museum of Art,
New York, Gift of Anni Albers
1970.75.26.

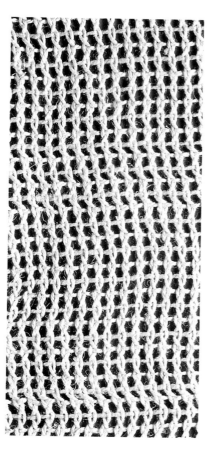

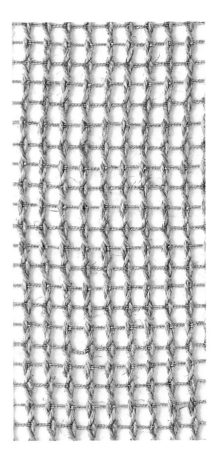

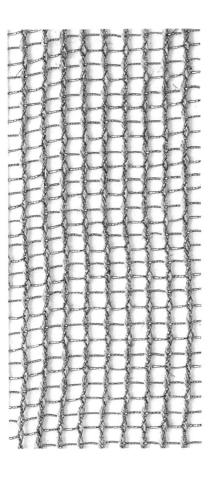

107. Textile sample, ca. 1951.
Jute and metallic thread,
21 × 17.7 cm (8¼ × 7 inches).
The Museum of Modern Art,
New York, Gift of Josef Albers
450.70.74.

108. Textile sample, ca. 1951.
Jute and metallic thread,
24.2 × 16.5 cm (9½ × 6½ inches).
The Museum of Modern Art,
New York, Gift of Josef Albers
450.70.72.

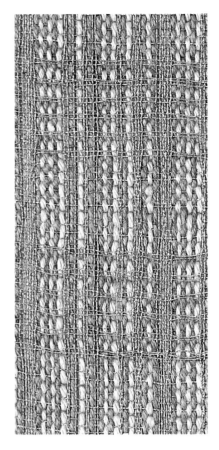

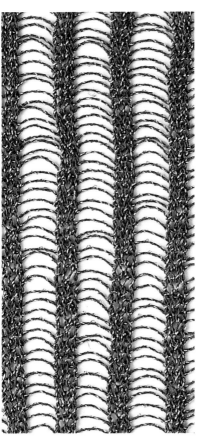

109. Wall-covering material,
probably after 1933.
Cotton and metallic thread,
27.9 × 11.4 cm (11 × 4½ inches).
The Museum of Modern Art,
New York, Gift of Josef Albers
450.70.66.

110. Casement material, 1950.
Cotton or synthetic and metal foil,
27.9 × 17.1 cm (11 × 6¾ inches).
The Museum of Modern Art,
New York, Gift of Josef Albers
450.70.80.

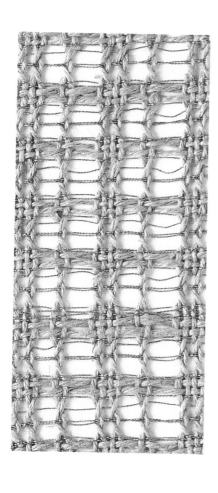

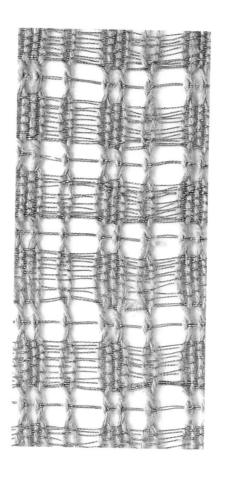

111. Textile sample, ca. 1951.
Linen and metallic thread,
25.4 × 17.8 cm (10 × 7 inches).
The Museum of Modern Art,
New York, Gift of Josef Albers
450.70.73.

112. Textile sample, ca. 1951.
Linen and metallic thread,
27.9 × 15.9 cm (11 × 6 ¼ inches).
The Museum of Modern Art,
New York, Gift of Josef Albers
450.70.79.

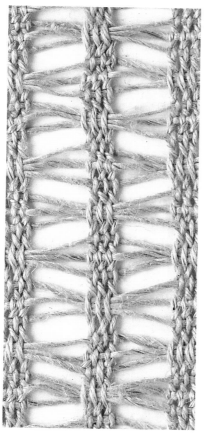

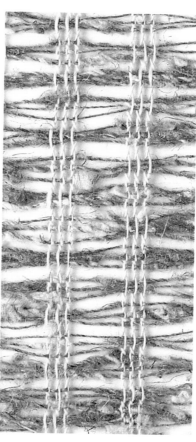

113. Textile sample, ca. 1933. Linen,
22.8 × 20.3 cm (9 × 8 inches).
The Museum of Modern Art,
New York, Gift of Josef Albers
450.70.70.

114. Textile sample, probably after
1933. Linen, 24.1 × 20.3 cm
(9 ½ × 8 inches). The Museum
of Modern Art, New York,
Gift of Josef Albers 450.70.71.

115. Textile sample, probably after 1933. Silk, 17.7 × 26.6 cm (7 × 10 ½ inches). The Museum of Modern Art, New York, Gift of Josef Albers 450.70.63.

116. Wall-covering material, ca. 1950. Jute and metallic thread, 29.2 × 12.7 cm (11 ½ × 5 inches). The Museum of Modern Art, New York, Gift of Josef Albers 450.70.65.

117. Wall-covering material, ca. 1950. Jute and metallic thread, 29.2 × 12.1 cm (11 ½ × 4 ¼ inches). The Museum of Modern Art, New York, Gift of Josef Albers 450.70.64.

118. Evening-coat material, 1946. Linen, cotton, and Lurex, 33 × 29.8 cm (13 × 11 ¾ inches). The Museum of Modern Art, New York, Gift of the designer 434.51.

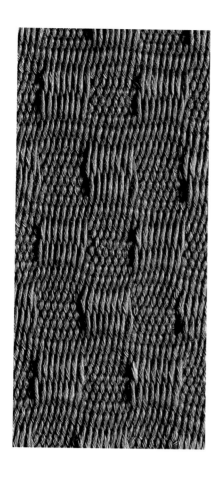

119. Textile sample, ca. 1948.
Harnessmaker's thread,
18 × 8 cm (7⅛ × 3⅛ inches).
The Metropolitan Museum of Art,
New York, Gift of Anni Albers
1970.75.77.

120. Textile sample, ca. 1948.
Harnessmaker's thread,
10.3 × 7.6 cm (4 1/16 × 3 inches).
The Museum of Modern Art,
New York, Gift of Josef Albers
450.70.100.

121. Textile sample, ca. 1948.
Harnessmaker's thread,
21.6 × 8.3 cm (8½ × 3¼ inches).
The Museum of Modern Art,
New York, Gift of Josef Albers
450.70.101.

122. Textile sample, ca. 1948.
Harnessmaker's thread,
15.9 × 8.2 cm (6¼ × 3¼ inches).
The Museum of Modern Art,
New York, Gift of Josef Albers
450.70.99.

123. Textile sample, probably after 1933. Cotton and metallic thread, 16.5 × 19 cm (6½ × 7½ inches). The Museum of Modern Art, New York, Gift of Josef Albers 450.70.81.

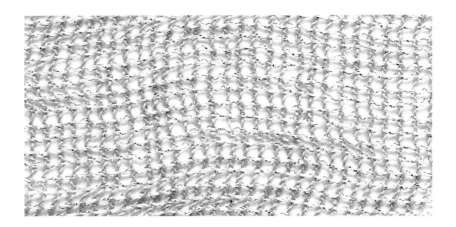

124. Textile sample, date unknown. Cotton and linen, 16 × 24 cm (6 5/16 × 9 7/16 inches). The Metropolitan Museum of Art, New York, Gift of Anni Albers 1970.75.42.

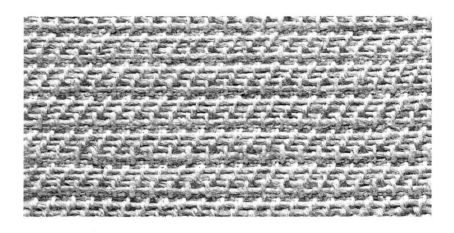

125. Upholstery material, 1929. Cotton and rayon, 11.4 × 19.7 cm (4½ × 7¾ inches). The Museum of Modern Art, New York, Gift of the designer 419.51.

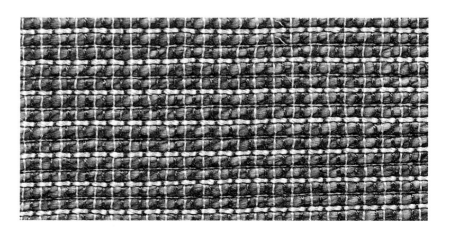

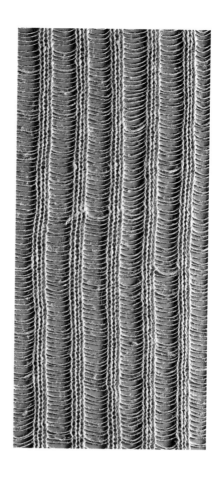

126. Knitted casement material, ca. 1960. Linen, 53 × 39 cm (20 ⅞ × 15 ⅜ inches). The Metropolitan Museum of Art, New York, Gift of Anni Albers 1970.75.22.

127. Wall-covering material, 1929. Designed for the auditorium of the Allgemeinen Deutschen Gewerkschaftsbundesschule, Bernau, Germany. Cotton and cellophane, 22.9 × 12.7 cm (9 × 5 inches). The Museum of Modern Art, New York, Gift of the designer 433.51.

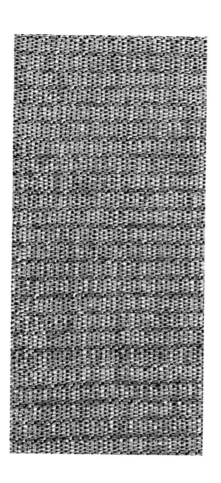

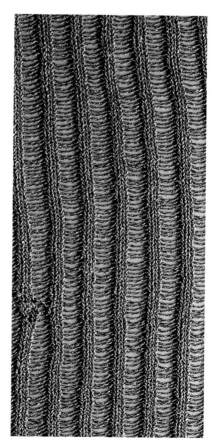

128. Knitted casement material, ca. 1960. Cotton and metallic thread, 57 × 35.5 cm (22 ⁷⁄₁₆ × 14 inches). The Metropolitan Museum of Art, New York, Gift of Anni Albers 1970.75.21.

129. Textile sample, date unknown. Cotton and linen, 28 × 21 cm (11 × 8 ¼ inches). The Metropolitan Museum of Art, New York, Gift of Anni Albers 1970.75.62.

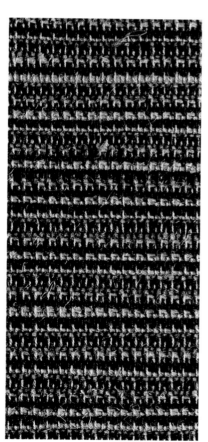

130. Textile sample, 1950.
Cotton and jute,
32.5 × 48 cm (12 ¾ × 18 ⅞ inches).
The Metropolitan Museum of Art,
New York, Gift of Anni Albers
1970.75.31a.

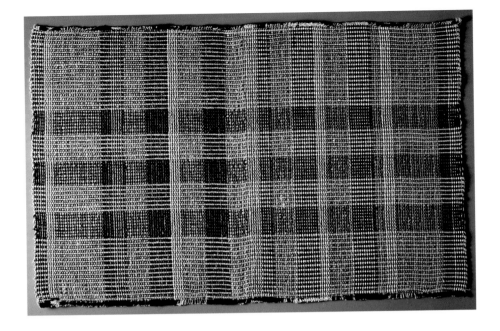

131. Textile sample, 1950.
Cotton and linen,
67.3 × 34 cm (26 ½ × 13 ⅜ inches).
The Metropolitan Museum of Art,
New York, Gift of Anni Albers
1970.75.34.

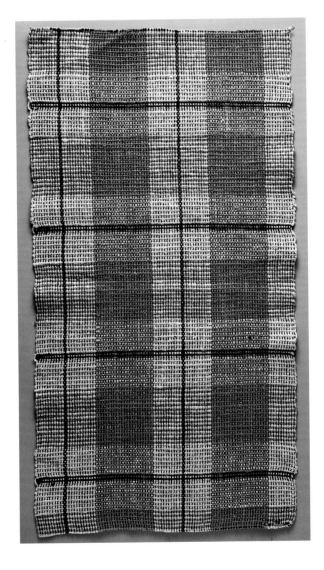

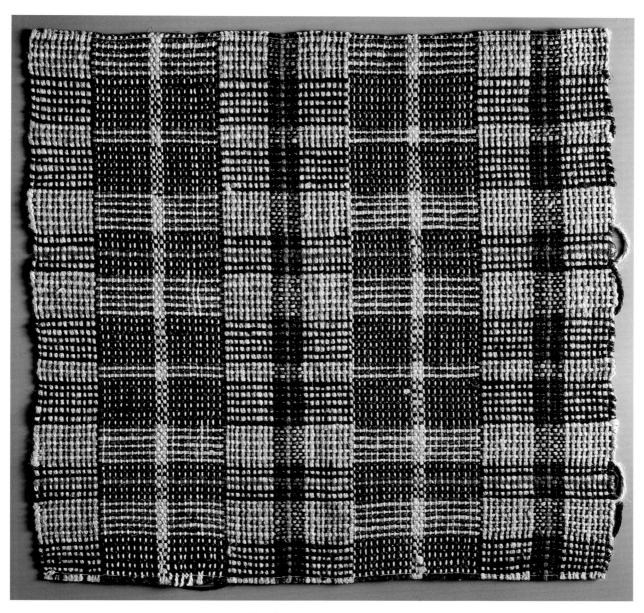

132. Textile sample, 1950.
Cotton and linen,
33 × 34 cm (13 × 13 ⅜ inches).
The Metropolitan Museum of Art,
New York, Gift of Anni Albers
1970.75.32.

Constructing Textiles

Anni Albers

Retrospection, though suspected of being the preoccupation of conservators, can also serve as an active agent. As an antidote for an elated sense of progress that seizes us from time to time, it shows our achievements in proper proportion and makes it possible to observe where we have advanced, where not, and where, perhaps, we have even retrogressed. It thus can suggest new areas for experimentation.

When we examine recent progress in cloth-making, we come to the curious realization that the momentous development we find is limited to a closely defined area . . . the creation of new fibres and finishes. While the process of weaving has remained virtually unchanged for uncounted centuries, textile chemistry has brought about far-reaching changes, greater changes perhaps than even those brought about through the fast advance in the mechanics of textile production during the last century. We find the core of textile work, the technique of weaving, hardly touched by our modern age, while swift progress in the wider area has acutely affected the quality as much as the quantity of our fabrics. In fact, while a development around the center has taken place, methods of weaving have not only been neglected, but some have even been forgotten in the course of time.

It is easy to visualize how intrigued, as much as mystified, a weaver of ancient Peru would be in looking over the textiles of our day. Having been exposed to the greatest culture in the history of textiles and having been himself a contributor to it, he can be considered a fair judge of our achievements. He would marvel, we can imagine, at the speed of mass production, at the uniformity of threads, the accuracy of the weaving and the low price. He would enjoy the new yarns used . . . rayon, nylon, aralac, dacron, orlon, dynel, and Fibreglas, to name some of the most important ones. He would admire the materials that are glazed or water-repellant, crease-resistant, permanent pleated, or flame-retarding, mothproof or shrinkage-controlled and those made fluorescent . . . all results of our new finishes. Even our traditionally used fabrics take on new properties when treated with them. He would learn with amazement of the physical as well as of the chemical methods of treating fabrics, which give them their tensile strength or their reaction to alkalis or acids, etc. Though our Peruvian critic is accustomed to a large scale of colors, he may be surprised to see new nuances and often a brilliance hitherto unknown to him, as well as a quantitative use of color surpassing anything he had imagined.

The wonder of this new world of textiles may make our ancient expert feel very humble and may even induce him to consider changing his craft and taking up chemistry or mechanical engineering. These are the two major influences in this great development, the one affecting the quality of the working material, and the other the technique of production. But strangely enough, he may find that neither one would serve him in his specific interest: the intricate interlocking of two sets of threads at right angles—weaving.

Concentrating his attention now on this particular phase of textile work, he would have a good chance of regaining his self-confidence. A strange monotony would strike him and puzzle him, we imagine, as he looked at millions of yards of fabric woven in the simplest technique. In most cases, he would recognize at one glance the principle of construction, and he would even find most of the more complex weaves familiar to him. In his search for inventiveness in weaving techniques, he would find few, if any, examples to fascinate him. He himself would feel that he had many suggestions to offer.

An impartial critic of our present civilization would attribute this barrenness in today's weaving to a number of factors. He would point out that an age of machines, substituting more and more mechanisms for handwork, limits in the same measure the versatility of work. He would explain that the process of forming has been disturbed by divorcing the planning from the making, since a product today is in the hands of many, no longer in the hands of one. Each member of the production line adds mechanically his share to its formation according to a plan beyond his control. Thus the spontaneous shaping of a material has been lost, and the blueprint has taken over. A design on paper, however, cannot take into account the fine surprises of a material and make imaginative use of them. Our critic would point out that this age promotes quantitative standards of value. Durability of materials, consequently, no longer constitutes a value per se and elaborate workmanship is no longer an immediate source of pleasure. Our critic would show that a division between art and craft, or between fine art and manufacture, has taken place under mechanical forms of production; the one carrying almost entirely spiritual and emotional values, the other predominantly practical ones. It is therefore logical that the new development should clarify the role of usefulness in the making of useful objects, paralleling the development of art, which in its process of clarification has divested itself of a literary by-content and has become abstract.

Though the weight of attention is now given to practical forms purged of elements belonging to other modes of thought, aesthetic qualities nevertheless are present naturally and inconspicuously. Avoiding decorative additions, our fabrics today are often beautiful, so we believe, through the clear use of the raw material, bringing out its inherent qualities. Since even solid colors might be seen as an aesthetic appendage, hiding the characteristics of a material, we often prefer fabrics in natural, undyed tones.

Our new synthetic fibres, derived from such different sources as coal, casein, soybeans, seaweed or lime have multiplied many times the number of our traditionally used fibres. Our materials therefore, even when woven in the simplest techniques, are widely varied in quality, and the number of variations are still increased through the effects of the new finishes. Yards and yards of plain and useful material, therefore, do not bore us. Rather they give us a unique satisfaction. To a member of an earlier civilization, such as our Peruvian, these materials would be lacking in those qualities that would make them meaningful to him or beautiful.

Though we have succeeded in achieving a great variety of fabrics without much variation of weaving technique, the vast field of weaving itself is open today for experimentation. At present, our industry has no laboratories for such work. (Today, 1959, the situation is changing.) The test tube and the slide rule have, so far, taken good care of our progress. Nevertheless, the art of building a fabric out of threads is still a primary concern to some weavers, and thus experimenting has continued. Though not in general admitted to the officialdom of industrial production, some hand-weavers have been trying to draw attention to weaving itself as an integral part of textile work.

At their looms, free from the dictates of a blueprint, these weavers are bringing back the qualities that result from an immediate relation of the working material and the work process. Their fresh and discerning attempts to use surface qualities of weaves are resulting in a new school of textile design. It is largely due to their work that textures are again becoming an element of interest. Texture effects belong to the very structure of the material and are not superimposed decorative patterns, which at present have lost our love. Surface treatment of weaving, however, can become as much an ornamental addition as any pattern by an overuse of the qualities that are organically part of the fabric structure.

Though it is through the stimulating influence of hand-weaving that the industry is becoming aware of some new textile possibilities, not all hand-weaving today has contributed to it. To have positive results, a work that leads away from the general trend of a period has to overcome certain perplexities. There is a danger of isolationism . . . hand-weavers withdrawing from contemporary problems and burying themselves in weaving recipe books of the past; there is a resentment of an industrial present, which due to a superior technique of manufacture, by-passes them;

there is a romantic overestimation of handwork in contrast to machine work and a belief in artificial preservation of a market that is no longer of vital importance.

Crafts have a place today beyond that of a backwoods subsidy or as a therapeutic means. Any craft is potentially art, and as such not under discussion here. Crafts become problematic when they are hybrids of art and usefulness (once a natural union), not quite reaching the level of art and not quite that of clearly defined usefulness. An example is our present day ash tray art . . . trash.

Modern industry is the new form of the old crafts, and both industry and the crafts should remember their genealogical relation. Instead of a feud, they should have a family reunion. Since the craft of weaving is making, in an unauthorized manner, its contribution to the new development and is beginning to draw attention to itself, we can look forward to the time when it will be accepted as a vital part of the industrial process.

The influence that hand-weaving has had thus far has been mainly in the treatment of the appearance, the epidermis, of fabrics. The engineering work of fabric construction, which affects the fundamental characteristics of a material, has barely been considered. It is probably again the task of hand-weavers to work in this direction. For just as silk, a soft material by nature, can become stiff in the form of taffeta, through a certain thread construction, and linen, a comparatively stiff material, can be made soft in another, so an endless number of constructional effects can produce new fabrics. The increasing number of new fibres incorporating new qualities creates a special challenge to try the effects of construction on them. Just as chemical treatment has produced fluorescence, so structural treatment can produce, for example, sound-absorption. Our ancient Peruvian colleague might lose his puzzled expression, seeing us thus set for adventures with threads, adventures that we suspect had been his passion.

Industry should take time off for these experiments in textile construction and, as the easiest practicable solution, incorporate hand-weavers as laboratory workers in its scheme. By including the weaver's imaginative and constructive inventiveness, as well as his land-loom with its wide operational scope, progress in textile work may grow from progress in part to a really balanced progress.

This essay originally appeared in "Constructing Textiles" *Design* 47:8 (April 4, 1946) and was reprinted in Alvin Lustig, ed. *Visual Communication* (New York, 1945) and in *Anni Albers: On Designing* (Wesleyan University Press: Middletown, Connecticut, 1971), pp. 12–16.

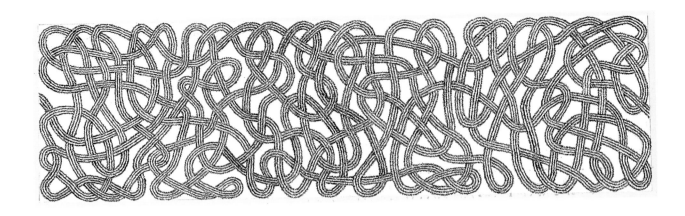

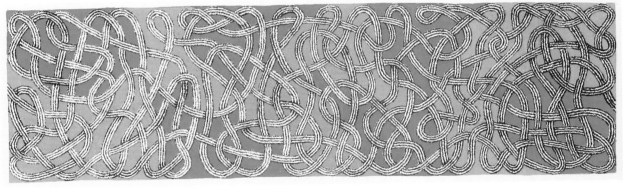

133. *Drawing for a Rug II*, 1959.
Ink and pencil on paper,
13.1 × 43.6 cm (5 ³⁄₁₆ × 17 ³⁄₁₆ inches).
The Josef and Anni Albers
Foundation, Bethany AA DR 013.

134. *Drawing for a Rug II*, 1959.
Gouache on paper,
13.1 × 43.6 cm (5 ³⁄₁₆ × 17 ³⁄₁₆ inches).
The Josef and Anni Albers
Foundation, Bethany AA DR 015.

135. *Drawing for a Rug II*, 1959.
Gouache on paper,
13.1 × 43.6 cm (5 ³⁄₁₆ × 17 ³⁄₁₆ inches).
The Josef and Anni Albers
Foundation, Bethany AA DR 016.

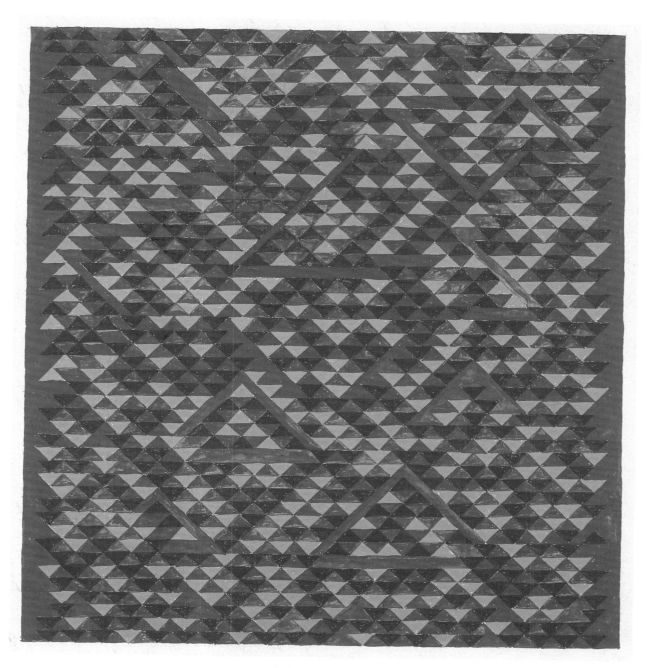

136. *Study for Camino Real*,
ca. 1967. Gouache on blueprint
paper, 29.7 × 27.6 cm
(11 ¹¹⁄₁₆ × 10 ⅞ inches).
The Josef and Anni Albers
Foundation, Bethany AA DR 021.

137. *Study for A*, 1968.
Gouache on graph paper,
27.9 × 26 cm (11 × 10 ⅜ inches).
The Josef and Anni Albers Foundation,
Bethany AA DR 024.

138. *Study for B*, 1968.
Gouache on graph paper,
31 × 23.8 cm (12 1/16 × 9 3/8 inches).
The Josef and Anni Albers Foundation,
Bethany AA DR 025.1

139. *DR XV B,* 1974. Ink on paper,
38.4 × 58.9 cm (15 ⅛ × 22 ⅜ inches).
The Josef and Anni Albers Foundation,
Bethany AA DR 053.

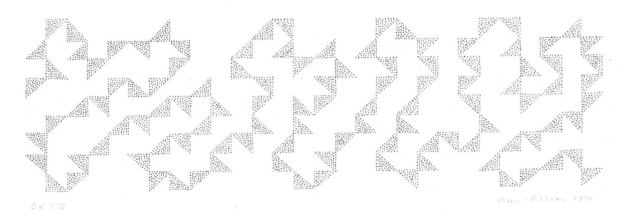

140. *DR XIV,* 1974. Ink on paper,
38.4 × 58.9 cm (15 ⅛ × 22 ⅜ inches).
The Josef and Anni Albers Foundation,
Bethany AA DR 051.

141. *Study for Triangulated Intaglio V,*
1976. Gouache on paper,
31.1 × 28.4 cm (12 ⁵⁄₁₆ × 11 ³⁄₁₆ inches).
The Josef and Anni Albers Foundation,
Bethany AA DR 070.

142. *Line Involvement II*, 1964.
Lithograph, 50.5 × 37.5cm
(19 ⅞ × 14 ¹³⁄₁₆ inches).
The Josef and Anni Albers Foundation,
Bethany AA PR 005/II.

143. *Line Involvement III*, 1964.
Lithograph, 37.5 × 50.5 cm
(14 ¹³⁄₁₆ × 19 ⅞ inches).
The Josef and Anni Albers Foundation,
Bethany AA PR 005/III.

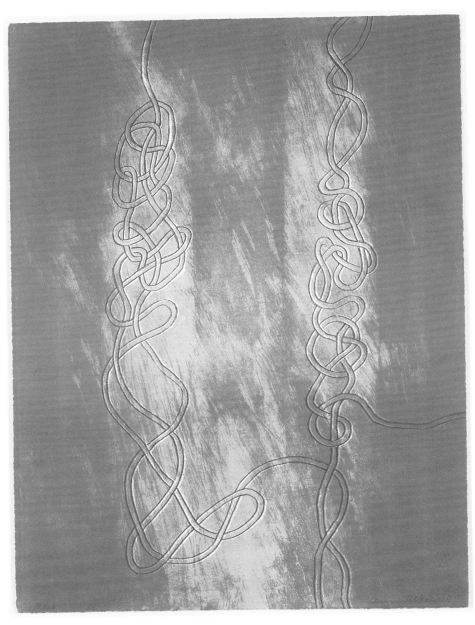

144. *Line Involvement IV*, 1964.
Lithograph, 50.5 × 37.5 cm
(19 ⅞ × 14 ¹³⁄₁₆ inches).
The Josef and Anni Albers Foundation,
Bethany AA PR 005/IV.

145. *Line Involvement V*, 1964.
Lithograph, 37.5 × 50.5 cm
(14 ¹³⁄₁₆ × 19 ⅞ inches).
The Josef and Anni Albers Foundation,
Bethany AA PR 005/V.

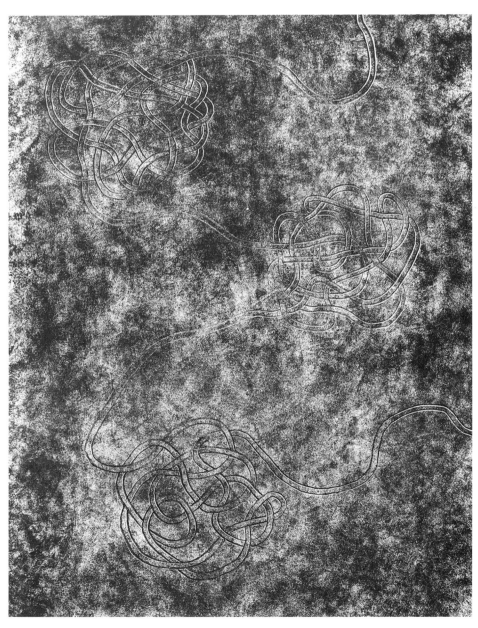

146. *Line Involvement VI*, 1964.
Lithograph, 50.5 × 37.5 cm
(19 ⅞ × 14 ¹³⁄₁₆ inches).
The Josef and Anni Albers Foundation,
Bethany AA PR 005/VI.

147. *Line Involvement VII*, 1964.
Lithograph, 50.5 × 37.5 cm
(19 ⅞ × 14 ¹³⁄₁₆ inches).
The Josef and Anni Albers Foundation,
Bethany AA PR 005/VII.

148. *Yellow Meander.* Screenprint,
71.1 × 61 cm (28 × 24 inches).
The Josef and Anni Albers Foundation,
Bethany AA PR 016.

149. *PO II*, 1973. Screenprint and photo-offset,
72.9 × 55.9 cm (28 11/16 × 22 inches).
The Josef and Anni Albers Foundation,
Bethany AA PR 034.

150. Anni Albers and Alex Reed,
Neck piece, ca. 1940.
Aluminum strainer, paper clips,
and chain; pendant:
10.8 × 8 cm (4 ¼ × 3 ⅛ inches).
Collection of Donna Schneier.

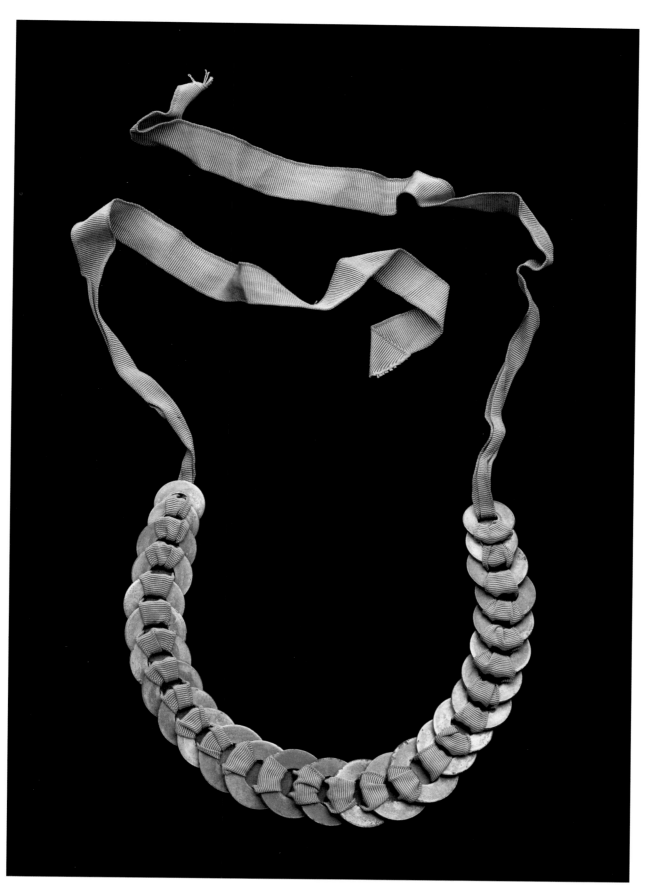

151. Anni Albers and Alex Reed,
Neck piece, ca. 1940.
Washers and grosgrain ribbon,
109.2 cm (43 inches) long.
Collection of Mrs. Barbara Dreier.

152. Anni Albers and Alex Reed,
Neck piece, 1988 reconstruction
of a ca. 1940 original.
Corks, bobby pins, and thread,
78.7 cm (31 inches) long.
Collection of Mary Emma Harris.

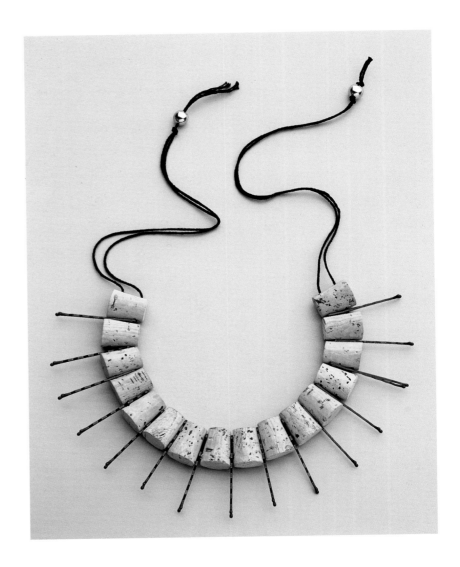

153. Anni Albers and Alex Reed,
Neck piece, ca. 1940.
Brass grommets and cotton cord,
83.8 cm (33 inches) long.
Collection of Mrs. Barbara Dreier.

154. Anni Albers and Alex Reed,
Neck piece, ca. 1940.
Brass grommets and chamois,
104.1 cm (41 inches) long.
Collection of Mrs. Barbara Dreier.

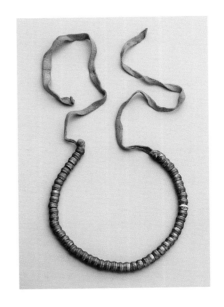

155. Anni Albers and Alex Reed,
Neck piece, 1988 reconstruction
of a ca. 1940 original.
Eye hooks, pearl beads, and thread,
83.8 cm (33 inches) long.
Collection of Mary Emma Harris.

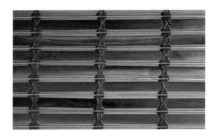

156. Free-hanging room divider,
ca. 1948. Walnut lath, dowels, and
waxed-cotton harnessmaker's thread,
326.4 × 108 cm (128½ × 42½ inches).
The Metropolitan Museum of Art,
New York, Gift of Anni Albers
1970.75.78.

157. Free-hanging room divider,
ca. 1949. Jute,
144.8 × 86.4 cm (57 × 34 inches).
The Museum of Modern Art,
New York, Gift of the designer
411.60.

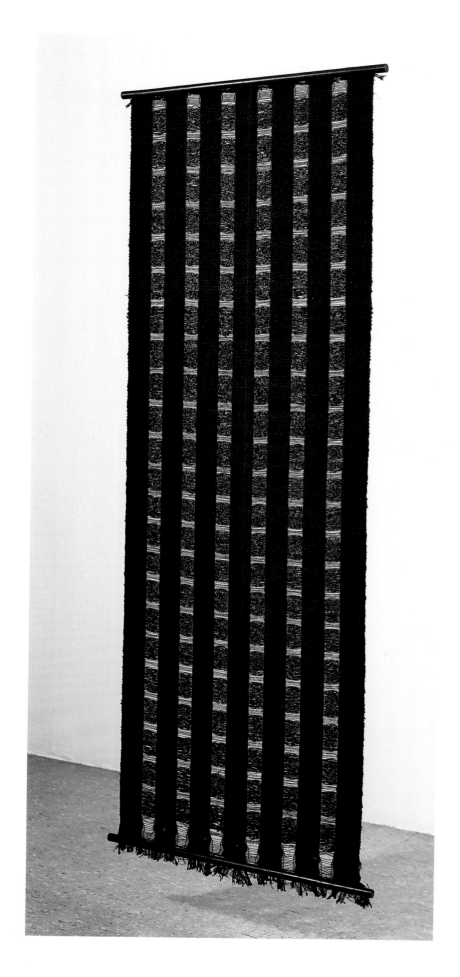

158. Free-hanging room divider, 1949. Cellophane and cord, 238.7 × 82.5 cm (94 × 32 ½ inches). The Museum of Modern Art, New York, Gift of the designer 409.60.

Anni Albers: Devotion to Material

Kelly Feeney

By all accounts, Anni Albers had never visited a synagogue before the mid-1950s, when the ark panels she designed for Temple Emanu-El in Dallas (figs. 160–61) were installed. Born to a family of assimilated Berlin Jews, Albers was baptized and confirmed in the Protestant church. This complex religious identity was a changeable feature of Albers's personality. Sometimes she was explicit about her background, particularly if she anticipated an affront. But on occasions she was quick to remind others that she was not Jewish (except, as she put it, "in the Hitler sense"), as in 1959, when the graphic designer Elaine Lustig Cohen asked Albers to weave a matzoh cover for her family's Passover seder. "You know I'm not Jewish," Albers replied, yet proceeded to carry out the assignment. One wonders if Albers sensed any irony in the Dallas commission, or in those she later received for other synagogue decorations and for a Holocaust memorial.[1]

In 1922 Albers left behind the upholstered comfort of her family's apartment in Berlin to attend the Bauhaus. Eleven years later, after the closing of the Bauhaus, she and her husband, Josef, left the uncertainties of Germany to teach at another experimental school, Black Mountain College, in the United States. During this tumultuous time Albers devoted herself to her art, as well as to teaching and writing about art. Her essays (for example, the 1939 text "Art—A Constant") often prescribe a devotional commitment. Clearly Modernism was Albers's religion, and her fervor for it overshadowed the complex relationship she had to Judaism.

In the mid-1950s the building committee of Temple Emanu-El hired the sculptor Gyorgy Kepes to oversee the interior decoration of its new synagogue, which had been designed by Howard Meyer and Max Sandfield. Kepes, who designed the sanctuary's pendant light fixtures and stained-glass windows himself, selected Albers for the design and fabrication of the ark covering.

Albers collaborated with Kepes on a fabric pattern that echoed not only his blue, green, and amber geometric window design, but the sparkling adobe-brick pattern of the sanctuary's main wall as well. Although Kepes had originally envisioned conventional ark curtains that could be drawn back to reveal the Torahs, Albers prevailed upon him to let her mount the material on sliding wooden panels. This solution, which Kepes accepted, typifies Albers's genius: fewer yards of the expensive custom fabric had to be spun, woven, and dyed, and, with the money saved, she was able also to design and produce a silvery material to line the back of the tabernacle.

The eight twenty-foot-high ark panels appear at first to be covered in a diverse mosaic of gold, green, and blue Lurex blocks. Albers, who

159. Study for Temple Emanu-El ark panels,
1957. Collage of colored paper, foil, textile
sample, and typewritten labels on paper,
43.1 × 36.2 cm (17 × 14 ⁵⁄₁₆ inches).
The Josef and Anni Albers Foundation,
Bethany AA DR 095.

was fluent in the language of geometry, achieved this effect by setting out an underlying modular structure in her fabric design; even though each panel bears the same pattern, the fabric is mounted at different points in the repeat or, on the center panels, simply turned upside down. This way, the spare roll of fabric that Albers supplied to the temple could be used to replace any one of the eight panels if damage were ever to occur.

Albers's rigorous aesthetic and practical economy transformed the synagogue's ark covering into a splendid architectural element. The panels are such a focal point in the sanctuary that the temple's building committee initially objected to them, even though they had approved the design several months earlier. In November 1956 the committee asked Kepes if Albers could produce a fabric pattern with "softened transitions"— to replace the fabric she had just made—in time for the synagogue's January dedication.[2] Albers informed Kepes that it would be impossible to meet that deadline, so the committee was forced to accept the panels as they were. But no one complained after the February 1957 issue of *Life* magazine came out, with the vast, glowing sanctuary reproduced in glorious color.[3]

Four years later the Congregation B'nai Israel of Woonsocket, Rhode Island, invited Albers to create an ark covering for their new temple, a baroque Modern building by Samuel Glaser. Albers responded with a work that is entirely different from the sleek, machine-woven piece she had made in Dallas, weaving six textured tapestries on a loom in her studio (fig. 162). As in Dallas, she mounted the textiles on wooden panels designed to slide apart during services. Measured amounts of gold Lurex in the tapestries lend luster to the other, much quieter, materials—cotton and jute—and make the textiles appear from a distance to be woven entirely of gold. On closer inspection the black and white lines of floating weft—which Albers referred to as "thread hieroglyphs"—emerge out of the general luminosity.[4] The B'nai Israel panels, which dominate the temple's sanctuary with a shimmering radiance, are somewhat calligraphic, symbolic of the sacred scriptures they protect and adorn.

In an unpublished statement about this commission, Albers wrote that an earlier weaving, which she described as "linear in design, vaguely suggesting written ciphers," was her point of departure.[5] (The earlier work is presumably *Black-White-Gold I* [1950, fig. 42].) This reference to "ciphers" relates to an ongoing theme in Albers's work: the implicit relationship between language and weaving. Albers's preoccupation with this idea grew out of a lifelong admiration for the weavings produced in pre-Conquest Peru, a culture that left behind extraordinary textiles but no written language. Albers believed that the "expressive directness" of the Andean weavers was possible precisely because they did not communicate through writing.[6] But Albers was also interested in the variety of visual forms that language can take. Among her papers (now held at the Josef and Anni Albers Foundation) are magazine clippings from the 1960s of various scripts, including Japanese calligraphy, musical notation, cuneiform, and Arabic, among others. She enjoyed the graphic qualities of these written languages and the mystery of their abstraction.

In the cipherlike design of the Woonsocket commission, Albers's interest in the written form intersected compellingly with a basic tenet of Judaism—the biblical injunction against iconography in favor of the study of Hebrew texts. The same is true of her subsequent commission, *Six Prayers*, for the Jewish Museum in New York (fig. 60). The Jewish

160 and 161. Ark panels,
Temple Emanu-El, Dallas, 1956
(open and closed).

Museum had begun in 1964 to acquire art memorializing the Jews who died in the Holocaust, after the philanthropist Vera List (the sister of Samuel Glaser) had established a special fund for this purpose. In 1965 Sam Hunter, the director-elect of the museum, wrote to Albers, inviting her to execute a commemorative tapestry. He stated that commissions were not being granted on the basis of religious faith or ethnic origin, and that the museum "placed no restrictions of any kind on the artistic character of the commissioned memorial, or upon its authorship."[7]

Albers worked for several months on the piece, gradually developing its format by weaving five full-scale studies.[8] In the spring of 1966, after she had submitted the finished tapestries and had received enthusiastic approval from the director, Hunter then hesitated to accept them. At the last minute he and List had noticed similarities between the work and her ark covering in Woonsocket. Hunter wrote to her, expressing his reservations: "It was our hope, of course, to have something quite unique as a memorial for the six million, and the existence of a work so similar would detract in my opinion from the uniqueness of this commission."[9] Albers responded to Hunter three days later.[10] In her letter she moderated what must have been a keen sense of disappointment, for by then she was sixty-seven years old and near the end of her weaving career, and this commission was clearly of enormous importance to her. She welcomed the comparison of *Six Prayers* to the earlier synagogue work but pointed out significant differences. In both works she had used six panels; but in Woonsocket she had set them close together to read as a unified whole, while in *Six Prayers* she had set them apart from one another, like stelae representing the six million dead. She also pointed out that the synagogue panels were a ceremonial, festive gold, in contrast to the monochromatic gray and silver of *Six Prayers*. She emphasized technical differences as well: for the ark panels, which she had woven in a matter of weeks, she had used a warp of loosely set cotton, while for *Six Prayers*, which she worked on over a period of several months, she had used a durable linen for both the closer-set warp and for most of the weft.

In the end, the museum overcame its reluctance and accepted *Six Prayers*. In a press release announcing the work's inaugural presentation, Albers wrote that the piece was conceived to be intimate rather than monumental.[11] Conducive to meditation, it has a palpable silence, the effect of Albers's characteristic poise and restraint. Yet the panels not only elicit prayer; they *are* a prayer, evoking loss and sorrow through their woven strands. Like the Peruvian textiles that Albers so admired, *Six Prayers* communicates outside any recognizable language. Its "thread-hieroglyphs," lit by silver, possess a subtle intensity; tugging at us, they slowly reveal their secrets.

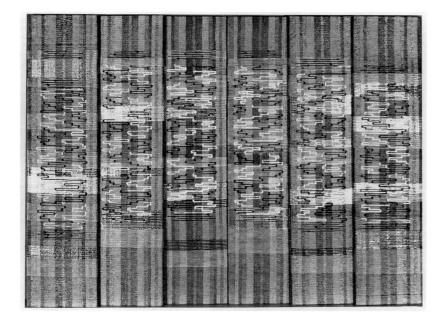

162. Ark panels, 1962.
Cotton, jute, and Lurex;
six panels, 162.6 × 213.4 cm
(64 × 84 inches) overall.
Temple B'nai Israel,
Woonsocket, Rhode Island.

Notes

1. Only the most significant of these commissions are discussed here. Apart from her commissions for Temple Emanu-El in Dallas, Temple B'nai Israel in Woonsocket, and the Jewish Museum in New York, Albers also created ark-curtain material for the Marcel Breuer–designed Scarsdale Reform Temple, Scarsdale, New York, in 1958, and a set of ark panels for the Congregation Hartzion Agudath Achim, Silver Springs, Maryland, in 1967. (The latter is now in the collection of the Israel Museum, Jerusalem.)

2. Howard Meyer and Max Sandfield, memorandum to the Temple Emanu-El Building Committee, Nov. 12, 1956, Temple Emanu-El, Dallas.

3. "Lofty Shrine: Dallas Congregation Dedicates Synagogue," *Life*, Feb. 25, 1957, p. 62.

4. Albers used the phrase "thread-hieroglyphs" in a letter to the Jewish Museum, March 26, 1966, The Josef and Anni Albers Foundation archives.

5. Anni Albers, unpublished manuscript, June 1962, The Josef and Anni Albers Foundation archives.

6. Anni Albers, *On Weaving* (Middletown, Conn.: Wesleyan University Press, 1965), p. 68. The titles of many of Albers's works refer explicitly to written language, such

as *Ancient Writing* (1936), *Pictographic* (1953), *Memo* (1958), *Open Letter* (1958), *Jotting* (1959), *Haiku* (1961), *Code* (1962), *Scroll* (1962), *Epitaph* (1968), and *Letter* (1980). For more on the relationship between language and Albers's weavings, see Virginia Gardner Troy's "Thread as Text: The Woven Work of Anni Albers" in this publication.

7. Sam Hunter, letter to Anni Albers, June 25, 1965, The Josef and Anni Albers Foundation archives.

8. Three of the five studies are in museum collections: Bauhaus-Archiv, Berlin; Art Institute of Chicago; and Weatherspoon Gallery, University of North Carolina, Greensboro. Another is in a private collection in Pittsburgh. The fifth has not been located.

9. Sam Hunter, letter to Anni Albers, March 23, 1966, The Josef and Anni Albers Foundation archives. Hunter had expressed enthusiasm in an earlier letter, dated Feb. 18, 1966, also in the Josef and Anni Albers Foundation archives.

10. Anni Albers, letter to Sam Hunter, March 26, 1966, The Josef and Anni Albers Foundation archives.

11. Press release, The Jewish Museum, New York, Jan. 1967, The Josef and Anni Albers Foundation archives.

The Last Bauhausler

Nicholas Fox Weber

Grasp the simple, embrace the primitive,
Diminish yourself, bridle your passions.
—Lao Tzú[1]

I.

When Anni Albers asked me if it would be possible to make fine-art prints at my family's commercial offset shop, she became a little girl eager to embark on a marvelous adventure. The eyes of this generally dour septuagenarian lit up with expectation. As when she had, at age twenty-two, embarked for the Bauhaus half a century earlier, she was entering her favorite realm: that of uncharted territory.

This austere woman, dressed in her inevitable whites and pale beiges, her graying hair sensibly cut, her only makeup a hint of lipstick and maybe some powder, sparkled like an eight-year-old in a party dress. Alice, perhaps: an unbridled enthusiast about to enter the magical kingdom.

It had not occurred to me that my family's printing company would offer anything to either of the artistic Alberses. Fox Press, some forty-five minutes from their house, mostly churned-out booklets and brochures for insurance and manufacturing companies; it was known for high-quality color-process printing, not for the sort of work that bears an artist's signature on each sheet in the tradition of limited-edition lithographs, etchings, and screenprints.

But Anni made her proposal with zeal. This great figure of Modernism—who would, by the end of her life, be the last surviving teacher of the Bauhaus—suggested it with the same eagerness and openness with which she entered the vast domain of her local Sears Roebuck (ten minutes from her house) and embarked on a course of what, with her lilting Berlin cadences, she enthusiastically called "tah-reasure hunting." At Sears she would extol the merits of plastic containers and polyester blouses, declaring that "all this emphasis on handmade" was nonsense, that machine processes were a wonderful thing, and that synthetics were among the marvels of our century.

I told Anni a bit about the technology of photo-offset. I gave a simple description that touched on the process in the most fundamental way—trying as best I could to follow Anni's patient and generous lead when, a few months earlier, she had led me to understand weaving by taking a Lord & Taylor box top and stretching lines of string from one end to the other and then inserting popsicle sticks at right angles to the string, with the sticks placed alternately above and below the taut fiber, in order to create a bare-bones loom that demonstrated warp and weft. She had told me then that she was delighted that someone so interested in her work—I was hoping, I had said, to write a book about it—knew nothing

163. Anni Albers, Milan, July 1983.

about textile technique, as she quite loathed "all that craft stuff" and wanted her work to be thought of as art first. I did not yet recognize the perverse aspects of her personality, but her wish to swim against the tide intrigued me, and since I thought Anni's "pictorial weavings" to have all the qualities of pure and great abstract art—to belong next to the paintings of her Bauhaus confreres Paul Klee and Vasily Kandinsky—and since I, too, had the arrogance to link most weaving with macramé and needlepoint and the like, I was amused and willing to follow her route.

When we began to discuss the possibility of her working with photo-offset, Anni proved to be a quick study. She decided that she would utilize the medium to make a print of two horizontal rectangular forms stacked one on top of the other. Each of the rectangles would contain a triangulated pattern, in keeping with the artist's recent geometric experimentations, a design full of diversion and ins and outs, but deliberately lacking in internal symmetry or repetition. At the Bauhaus, Anni had been deeply moved by Wilhelm Worringer's pivotal book *Abstraction and Empathy*; she embraced Worringer's idea of abstraction providing the opportunity to create "visual resting places" removed from the often painful realities of the natural world. She was interested in art that was timeless and universal rather than art with specific links to a known locale or moment in history—or to the maker's personal experience. This pure realm of art could provide some of the harmony that life itself sometimes lacked. To keep the viewer engaged, the new creation, like all of Anni's compositions, had to eschew easy resolution; like Josef, Anni imbued abstraction with a certain tension, a perpetual in/out motion, an ongoing play between image and ground. The artist's own persona was to fade in deference to the sacred realm of art and the comforts as well as the realities of the technical. Anni had no wish to reveal private emotions or the sometimes troubling fluctuations of her own mind and heart; she preferred, instead, to focus on the purely aesthetic and practical issues of printmaking, just as she had for many years reveled in the construction of textiles. It is no wonder that Lao Tzú's words were so beloved by Anni, who kept a volume of his philosophy in perpetual reach at her bedside.

Photo-offset, she determined, would enable her to reproduce her own deliberately irregular pencil strokes, and simultaneously to obtain the crystalline edges and reversals allowed by machine technology. The photographic reproduction of her gray markings had never been possible in the print mediums with which she had previously worked—lithography, etching, and screenprinting. It enabled her to suggest mysterious, and musical, communication of the sort that fascinated her in hieroglyphics and other ancient forms of writing. She liked nonspecific language, the idea of a voice being heard even if the precise meaning of its intonations was indecipherable. In contrast to the gray, a red pattern that had been hand-cut on a rubylith—a bright plastic sheet of two layers—in the stripping department from an original sketch by Anni was to be printed opaquely on the top half of this two-section print, while the pattern was to be reversed on the lower half. What was red above was gray below, and vice versa, another result of the photo-mechanical process. The solids above were pencil strokes below; the pencil above unmodulated red below.

The irregularity of her pencil strokes—this elusive fuzziness—against the crisp purity of machined forms appealed to her. So did the idea that, with a flick of the wrist, she could make what was negative in one rectangle positive in the other. She was grateful to the technology for having opened new visual possibilities—as if it, not she, was the responsible party. Now she could achieve the sort of contrast and unpredictability, the

164. *Fox I*, 1973. Photo-offset,
38 × 34 cm (14 ⅞ × 13 ⁷⁄₁₆ inches).
The Josef and Anni Albers Foundation,
Bethany.

165. *Fox II*, 1973. Photo-offset,
38 × 34 cm (14 ⅞ × 13 ⁷⁄₁₆ inches).
The Josef and Anni Albers Foundation,
Bethany.

mixture of the personal and the impersonal, the coincidence of order and spontaneity, and hence the playfulness and elements of surprise intrinsic to her work—while being part of the modern world.

A year or so later—when I began to write in some detail about Anni's life and work—she would tell me, in the confessional tone of a rebel Communist letting you know that she had grown up with finger bowls in the house, that, like so many abstractionists, she had started out with very traditional renditions of the natural world in her work. (Unfortunately, none of the evidence remains.) The first art teacher of Annelise Fleischmann (she would shorten her first name when she took Josef's as her last), when she was about ten and still being educated in a small group of children with tutors, was a Miss Violet—Anni loved the name—for whom she painted "some good naturalistic watercolors of little autumn leaves."[2] Then, when she was fourteen and had enrolled in the lyceum, her parents hired a private art teacher, Toni Mayer, who came once a week to the house with a nude model for Anni to draw. In retrospect, the idea of the figure drawing she had done as a young woman made little sense to Anni, but at the time it made her "feel very professional," and she was excited by the way that the progressive and liberated "Tonuschka" gave her "a first look at the world beyond bourgeois Berlin." At age fifteen, in 1914, Anni made as her entry to a lyceum competition for posters to give to World War I orphans "a picture of short-haired little girls sitting behind each other in a row. Each wore a skirt about three inches short of her knees and was knitting, with a ball of wool in front of her." Could Anni have had a premonition of her future involvement with thread? Did she realize that with that image she was combining her role of star pupil with that of bête noir? She got word that the posters were unacceptably immodest, the skirts too brief. A poster she considered distinctly inferior won first prize, while hers was awarded only an honorable mention. Her frustration over this—Anni always seemed to take a certain pleasure in having been wronged—was still with her over half a century later.

With her next art teacher, she continued both working figuratively and breaking the rules. Now a full-time art student with the Postimpressionist Martin Brandenburg, whom she liked and from whose strict discipline she felt she benefited even if she questioned the specifics of his training, she made representational paintings about half life-size. The problems began when, "having seen a beautiful Lucas Cranach Eve painted against a black background"—one must imagine the sonorous, soft voice and deliberate speaking manner, the subtle but distinct emphasis on the word "beautiful," its first syllable stretched warmly—she began, in violation of Brandenburg's recommended technique, to put black in her paintings. Brandenburg said that if she did not abandon this use of black she could not return to his classes. Anni was in tears. Her mother arranged a reconciliation, the rebellious student vowing to comply with the teacher's dictates, but the work she produced after that time makes clear how much she ultimately delighted in that black.

When Anni first gave me the sketch for the pattern to be made in solid red, I instructed the stripper to simulate her handwork exactly. My erroneous assumption was that in the outlines she would want the same sort of personal effect that the gray pencil strokes had. It took the stripper days to cut a rubylith that perfectly resembled her drawing—only to have Anni respond by saying that she hated the handmade appearance. She meant her drawing only as a guide to the design and desired exact, crisp lines and sharply pointed triangles with the points just lightly touching. The stripper then developed a grid from which he cut the triangles precisely; since the bottom unit was simply the reverse of the top, all he had to do was cut one piece.

Once all the preparatory stages were complete—this process had taken many months, during which my regular visits to the Alberses had exposed me, with thrilling intimacy, to a more honest and intense devotion to art than I had ever thought possible—Anni said that she wanted to make a trip to Fox Press. She needed, she felt, to watch the actual printing in order to determine the intensity of the gray as it rolled off the press and to make sure that the opaque red trapped it exactly, containing the pencil without any unwelcome white space around it.

We agreed that I would pick her up one morning at the modest, shingled, raised ranch house where she and Josef lived on a pleasant suburban street in the town of Orange, fifteen minutes from the center of New Haven. Although she still drove short distances on her own, it was better for me to take her on the hour-long journey to Fox Press, which was on the north side of Hartford, and return her at the end of the day.

In those days I drove an MG roadster, which I thought would be impossible for Anni to get into. She walked awkwardly, often using a cane, and her legs and feet seemed slightly malformed. I did not yet know what her precise disability was, but she had terribly thin calves—there had been an incorrect rumor at Black Mountain College that she had contracted rickets during World War I—and she wore large custom-made shoes that were clearly designed to accommodate a structural problem. Anni had once referred to having remained seated at Bauhaus parties while Josef danced all night, and at another point had mentioned that she had broken her hip a few years earlier, but she never identified the actual problem. (I would later learn from her brother, Hans Farman, that Anni, like her mother, suffered from a genetic syndrome that caused them to have an extreme arch in both feet, as a result of which their leg muscles could not fully develop. Anni's sister, Lotte, and Hans both feared that their children might be similarly afflicted—they were not—and Hans presumed that it was one of the reasons that Anni and Josef had never had children of their own. Indeed, Charcot-Marie-Tooth disease, the hereditary progressive nerve disorder from which Anni suffered, would probably have caused any female children she had to have the same sort of clawed feet, nerve deterioration, and wasting of leg muscles as Anni had.[3] Other people, however, said that the reason was that the Alberses' work *was* their children, and that their involvement with their art left no time or energy for family matters.) So for the sake of Anni's comfort I drove my mother's Rover sedan, which so fascinated Josef that he came outside to the driveway to study it.

Josef paced back and forth analyzing the English car. It was similar, he said, to their Mercedes, in that, unlike American designs, neither of these models wasted trunk space. The importance of this relationship of form and function was never minimized. The Alberses had already told me on many occasions that they preferred their Polaroid camera and portable Sony television to the paintings of the Abstract Expressionists. Clean and effective design with a purpose ranked far higher than art focused on the revelation of one's private self.

Anni evinced the same pleasure embarking on our outing as she had over our collaboration from the start. Clearly she liked the attention, the eagerness of a young man to cater to her whims and soak up her views. And I was content beyond belief; after years of studying art history, in

166. Josef Albers at 8 North Forest Circle, New Haven, Connecticut, ca. 1968.

both Anni and Josef I had encountered, as never before, people who genuinely lived and breathed art as the essence of their lives. For the Alberses art was the central issue—not on the periphery as it was in most institutions of American education and in our culture at large. The visual world was supreme for each of them individually, and in their marriage.

In the preceding months Anni and I had established a remarkable rapport. Josef and I often had wonderful conversations—about Giotto's line as opposed to Duccio's, about German Rococo architecture, about the fraudulence of most of America's famous artists—but Anni was the more accessible of the two of them, eager to cross the line from discussing topics to establishing an intimate personal connection. Josef was entirely content with his work and sense of self; Anni needed friends. In this arena she was as selective as in all of her other choices, but once one had made it to the inner sanctum, there was much pleasure in being there, even if one had to remain somewhat on guard and on good behavior. Arrogant, imperious, demanding, and snobby, this highly intelligent woman, this grand duchess of Modern art, could be as gracious and charming, genuinely so, as she could be dismissive. It was, of course, flattering to be among the few who escaped her opprobrium: I recognized the rarity of the position and savored it as such.

In fact, it was Josef who initially latched onto the significance of my coming from the world of printing. What in my mind seemed too ordinary and bourgeois and businesslike for people like the Alberses was to them laden with rare potential. The occasion was our very first meeting, in 1971. I was then a twenty-three-year-old graduate student in art history at Yale. My friend Ruth Agoos—who with her husband, Herb, collected both Anni's and Josef's work, and who had been, to the cool and distant extent to which the Alberses jointly permitted personal relationships to develop, a friend of theirs for over a decade—had asked me to accompany her in calling on them. At that point I was familiar with Josef's work and reputation but knew very little about his wife's other than the pieces by her I had seen at the Agooses'. It was Josef whom I anticipated meeting.

I did not quite know what to expect from the great painter and color theorist who had now made such a mark on American art—Josef had, a year earlier, been the first living artist ever to have a major retrospective at the Metropolitan Museum of Art in New York—but I was properly nervous and intimidated in advance. I donned my one clean pair of corduroys, a herringbone jacket, and a tie—I would later discover how right I was in having a foreboding that such details counted in a major way where I was going—and did my utmost to keep the grease off my pants when I had to get underneath the MG to bang the fuel pump with a rock. By the time Ruth and I pulled up at the Alberses' house, at 808 Birchwood Drive, I was past being flapped—at least the car had finally started—but I could not help being astonished by the blatant ordinariness—in fact, the ugliness—of the house, with its shingles the color of Band-Aids and its strident concrete foundation completely devoid of planting. In my mind, I had expected to arrive at a pavilion by Walter Gropius, or at least something sleek and white and edged in chrome, not a satellite from Levittown.

But the moment we went up the half-flight of stairs and, in an interior more austere and minimal and spare than anything one would ever find in Levittown, met the Alberses, their presence—it was a mutual presence, more than the impression of two separate beings—filled the space completely. Josef was stocky, of medium height, and had a large head—his build was almost like Picasso's, but without the musculature—while Anni, who was tall for a woman, was thin as a rail. But whatever their builds, they were truly *big* people; they animated the world around them. The nearly empty house, with its few pieces of lean furniture and complete absence of personal objects, its walls practically blank save for four paintings by Josef and work by two of his students (nothing by Anni was in sight), was like a minimal Modern stage set occupied by characters of Shakespearean dimensions.

The redness of Josef's skin seemed accentuated by the snow-whiteness of his smooth, straight hair, precisely the sort of color effect he would have remarked on in his teaching. Anni, although she would later tell me that she was so dark-skinned that she had been able to take lots of sun without any problem during their visits to Mexico in the era before sunscreens were readily available while the fairer Josef had had to protect himself assiduously, made a paler impression—like a figure in a black-and-white movie slightly out of focus and infused with light. I regret to say that she had something about her that reminded me of Olive Oyl of Popeye comic book fame, but if this was less than flattering to her looks, the Olive Oyl–like mix of awkwardness and amiability, the apparent receptiveness and eager gaze at me as a newcomer, won me over.

"What do you do, *boy*?" Josef asked me in a strident voice only seconds after Ruth had introduced us and I had been struck by the strength and control with which the rugged octogenarian had shaken my hand.

"I study art history at Yale, sir," I answered—reduced, as I was, to some lower echelon: a student before a senior professor, an apprentice before a master, a private before a general.

"Do you like it, *boy*?" This was not someone who believed in pussyfooting.

I had no idea what his relationship with the university was, and I was greatly dependent on the monthly stipends awarded as part of my fellowship grant; I thought he might have the power to send me packing in an instant. But I have always been one to declare the truth at whatever cost, and if he wouldn't mince words, neither would I.

"No, sir, I . . . really . . . don't."

"Why *not, boy*?"

"Well, sir, I find that I'm losing my passion for looking at art. I mean, this past semester I've been taking a course called 'Seurat and the Iconography of Entertainment,' and for the past three weeks I've been in a library basement studying gas-lighting fixtures in nineteenth-century France to understand the details of *Le Chahut*. When I tried to talk to the teacher about what the painting looked like, about the colors and forms, or how it was made, he said that that wasn't the subject of the course. Now when I go to museums I think so much about all the facts they're looking for that I find I can't feel that inexplicable thrill of the art anymore."

I noticed that Anni was looking at me with what I deduced was a degree of fascination, and with what seemed an approving if quizzical smile.

"This I like, *boy*," Josef declared, as, to my complete surprise, he put his arm around me and patted my back. "Which of those bastards in art history don't you like?"

I answered, and we bandied about the names of a few of the professors in the department. Anni now chimed in. They had the usual disdain that practicing artists hold for art historians. She referred to one well-known professor as being—she grinned like a little kid as she used the American idiom—"full of hot air."

"And what does your father do?" Josef then asked. The question puzzled me slightly. I had not expected it—I was past defining myself by my parents' professions—and it was only months later that I realized

167. Josef Albers at 8 North Forest Circle, New Haven, Connecticut, 1968, photographed by Henri Cartier-Bresson.

to what extent Josef always emphasized *his* father's occupation. Lorenz Albers had been a housepainter who also did carpentry, electrical work, and plumbing; Josef had the deepest admiration for the practical skills, the emphasis on technical proficiency and knowledge of materials, he had learned as a child. "I come from Adam and my father. That's all," he would declare resolutely to scholars who pointed to the glass artist Johan Thorn-Prikker (with whom Josef had apprenticed before attending the Bauhaus) or to Vincent van Gogh, or, less accurately, to the German Expressionists as a source for his early style and subsequent developments.

Besides, my mother was a painter; I thought perhaps that the Alberses might be interested that I grew up in a house with a studio in it, that the whiff of oil paint I detected in their living room was the same as the one I had known throughout my childhood.

But I answered the question as asked. "He's a printer. I mean, he owns a printing company."

"Good," Josef replied, smiling. "Then you know something about something. You're not just an art historian." I felt at that moment as if Anni had been looking at me first with the nervousness, then the relief, of a girl whose date has just met her father for the first time, and who has gotten through the first round all right. What I did not yet realize was that my answer had afforded her a certain comfort, since her father had also owned his own company, and in effect we came from similar backgrounds—for which her word of choice would have been "bourgeois." Her father was a furniture manufacturer—a line of work similar to printing in its combination of business and aesthetic concerns. For Anni, who by nature felt isolated, this link between us had meaning.

From that point forward, Josef talked to me often about the graphic arts—he esteemed graphic design as an art form, had worked with many interesting printers, and had designed several alphabets—and gave me various materials pertaining to the subject.

Meanwhile, Anni, who had had far less to say in that first conversation, had obviously begun to hatch a scheme. While Josef had been interested in my printing connection theoretically, she recognized some more tangible possibilities in the relationship. She might make something at the different sort of printing company my family owned. And in the young man who had been brought in that afternoon, she might have both a friend and an admirer. She was, I discovered in time, deeply in need of both.

What I most remember of the rest of that initial encounter was that Anni and Ruth and I went out, with Anni driving her Chevrolet station wagon, to procure lunch, and that I learned that when you see the world through the eyes of one of the earliest proponents of the Bauhaus, the mass production and efficiency of Kentucky Fried Chicken takes on a new dimension, and that when someone of Anni's distinction and elegance makes a pronouncement like "Josef and I don't like extra kah-rispy," it has a magic that such preferences lack when uttered by more ordinary souls. I also came to see that day that even the least appealing of fast foods takes on a new charm when enunciated in quiet Berlin tempo— "Ken-tucky fah-ried"—and served on immaculate white Rosenthal china from a spare and lean rolling cart, arranged there by someone whose eyes and unerring design sense govern every slight decision.

It was two years later that I was driving Anni to Fox Press. She gave to her entrance to the printing plant the same very individual magic, the deliberateness and quirky charm, that she lent to most simple actions.

Proportioned like one of Alberto Giacometti's striding figures and walking with the aid of her plain stick, Anni was striking both for the dignity of her dark brunette hair and her stately manner. By her own definition, she "purposefully avoided an arty look"—a bent she shared with Josef, who was most often seen in solid-colored, straight-collared shirts and khaki or gray wool trousers; the tone set by their clothing was of considerable importance to both the Alberses. For her Fox Press outing, Anni wore a simply cut, rather severe khaki skirt that ended just below the knee, a silky white crepe blouse, and a pure-white cable-stitch sweater. Not yet knowing her well, I assumed that the sweater was expensive, handmade, and imported—that someone of Anni Albers's stature would wear nothing else—but having become more closely acquainted with her I have come to realize that it was probably machine-made, synthetic, and washable—and from a discount store. For I now know that she always preferred the practical products of mass production to most luxury goods—and regularly instructed weavers championing the handmade and belittling machine work to look at their own shirts.

Anni's plain, mostly inexpensive clothes acquired a rare elegance on her, in part because of the way they fit and hung; her suits from Alexander's (a department store noted for its cheap merchandise) might have been Chanels. (When asked whom she considered to be the greatest artist of the twentieth century, she was inclined to answer "Coco Chanel.") Along with the whites and tans that day, Anni had on a brown suede jacket, a shimmering brown scarf, and heavy brown suede shoes; the balances were of color as well as of texture.

When we walked into the pressroom, I told Anni that when my father had built Fox Press, he had considered buying *Standing Lithographer* by David Smith, a seven-and-a-half-foot-tall figure with a steel type case for a chest. I lamented this with the collector's usual woe over the art masterpiece almost bought, explaining that the ten thousand dollars needed to buy it had ended up being required for a fire door. (The Smith had recently sold for one hundred and seventy thousand dollars, a detail I considered too vulgar to mention but of which I was keenly aware.) Anni was surprisingly unmoved by what I considered a misfortune. Without missing a beat, she simply pointed to a large Swiss two-color press in front of us and declared, "You see that machine? *That*, that is far more beautiful than anything David Smith ever touched."

Anni positioned herself carefully on a wooden chair next to the thirty-two-inch single-color press where her print was to be run. She exuded a sense of importance and rectitude, as well as grace, but was mercifully free of the self-consciousness of a grande dame. She was, quite simply, an honest worker trying to do her job as best she could. There was nothing of an old lady about her; she was neither a "character" nor a "person of importance," and her age and gender assumed minor roles. What was remarkable was her quiet brilliance, and her humility alongside her complete originality. As the pressman adjusted the press, she spoke of the wonder of the machine and of the artist's need to respond to the capabilities of the equipment.

Anni was curious about the flexible plate that was being locked onto a roller and wanted to know more about how it was made. The pressman fetched the platemaker, who suggested that we go into the prep department to see how it was created. Observing the chemical processes and fit of the halftones, Anni marveled at the accuracy of mechanization. As she exulted in the technology, this woman who at the Bauhaus had worked alongside Klee and Kandinsky fifty years earlier, somehow made this printing plant in Connecticut an outgrowth of Bauhaus thinking and life. What she evoked of that great and pioneering art school was not its complicated politics or the rivalries that sometimes sullied its atmosphere, but rather its crisp thinking and marriage of creativity and technology.

While impressively humble in her demeanor, she had a degree of politeness that suggested the true ranks of noblesse. Shaking hands with the men at the plant, Anni smiled graciously and told them that she admired what they did. "Craft people," Anni complained to me in an aside, suffered from their inability to use machines; they should simply look at what they were wearing to understand the value of mechanization. It was yet another reiteration of this favorite point.

Watching the first few prints roll off the press, which was usually used to fire off brochures by the thousands, Anni was riveted—as she had been while the parts were clamped into place and the rollers inked. This was consistent with the passion for preparation and process that she had often voiced to me. As a child of ten, when she went to the symphony with her sister, both in their black velvet dresses with white Irish lace collars, her favorite moment had always been that of the orchestra tuning up—more than the actual performance. When her parents gave costume parties in their Berlin apartment, she loved watching the usual furniture being taken away and the party props being moved in, just as she was fascinated by the return to the norm after the party; transformation, and the working of components, were her nectar. The end result was never quite as interesting. But what pleasure there had been on the occasion in her childhood when her family's formal flat became the Grunewald, the vast area of parks on the outskirts of Berlin. Large canvases of landscapes were specially installed to create this picnic setting, and guests entering the verdant paradise were met by a simulated boat, created on a bed frame on wheels, that ferried them a few feet through the entryway, as if they were crossing one of the lakes of the Grunewald. Mostly Anni had negative memories of her mother; she mainly recalled confrontation (even though her mother had arranged all the study of art when the adolescent Anni showed some initial talent, and had accompanied her to the studio of Oskar Kokoschka in Dresden in the hopes that he would take her on as a pupil—he did not) and her mother's complaints and pessimism. But she fondly remembered the occasion when her mother appeared at a party where the motif was a railroad station—established by murals of sausage stands, ticket booths, and information desks—and acted like a child who was lost before returning as a mother looking for a missing child.

Variations outside the norm, the shifts from one state to another, the sense of something happening: these brought considerable delight to Anni and Josef. On those occasions when I drove them to New York, they were invariably fascinated by construction sites and the scaffolding of new buildings, pointing out to me how the process evolved.

Trial and error—the essence of process—never seemed to frustrate Anni. By the time of our visit to the print shop, she had had to redo the handmade pencil part of her print at least twice before we discovered that these grays units had to be larger than she intended them to be in the final print so that they could be totally trapped, as Anni wished them to be, by the solid design on top. Now, as the first prints began to roll off the press, Anni saw that the gray of the upper half was darker than at the bottom. She insisted that this was her fault; she had done the two parts on separate occasions and had applied too little pressure the second time. As with her work in weaving, certain issues were paramount: the knowledge of materials, the degree of force or laxity, the wish for deliberate balance

168. Annelise (right) and Lotte Fleischmann, Berlin, ca. 1908.

as a setting for irregularity, and the adjustments required to proceed from the initial concept to an end result that was still completely fresh.

The foreman joined the pressman in discussing the problem of the two differing grays and Anni's wish to regulate them. They determined that a press adjustment would enable them to lighten the top gray. Anni was thrilled to use the machine to correct her mistake. She explained to all of us that the printing was as important to her artwork as was her initial design concept. The role of the equipment, she subsequently told me, had been equally important when she started textile work at age twenty-two. Initially she had resisted the medium and had considered it "sissy stuff"—she used the term often—as opposed to wall painting or the other Bauhaus workshops she had hoped to enter. As her entrance projects by which she had gained admission to the Bauhaus, she had made a three-dimensional study out of the interiors of thermos bottles—broken bits of glass and metal—and a very naturalistic drawing of a piece of wood accompanied by a black-to-white color sequence. Not unnaturally in light of the thermos assemblage, once she was admitted she considered entering the stained-glass workshop, where she admired the skill and originality of the glass-shard collages being made by Josef, eleven years her elder and one of the reasons that, in spite of having failed her initial entrance exam, she had become so eager to remain at the Bauhaus. (Josef coached her for the second round of tests, which she passed.) But the Bauhaus masters felt that one person was enough in that field—and that carpentry, wall painting, or metalwork would prove to be too strenuous for her. She told me, "I was not at all enthusiastic about going into the weaving workshop, because I wanted to do a real man's job and not something as sissy as working with threads." But once she accepted the idea of textiles, she immersed herself in the possibilities and limitations of the loom, the textures of the available materials, the role of warp and weft, and the visible charms as well as the structural aspect of knotting. "Even if you were a painting student of Klee's or Kandinsky's, you had to go through a course in a workshop. So I had to do that if I wanted to stay; and I wanted to stay. This weaving was a kind of railing to me—the limitations that come with a craft. That was a tremendous help to me, as I think it probably can be to anybody, so long as you, at the same time, are concerned with breaking through it."

II.
I knew a man once who was the best compositor in the world, and who was sought out by all those who devoted themselves to inventing artistic types; he derived joy, not so much from the very genuine respect in which he was held by persons whose respect was not lightly bestowed as from the actual delight in the exercise of his craft, a delight not wholly unlike that which good dancers derive from dancing. I have known also compositors who were experts in setting up mathematical type, or script, or cuneiform, or anything else that was out of the way or difficult. I did not discover whether these men's private lives were happy, but in their working hours their constructive instincts were fully gratified.
—Bertrand Russell[4]

A month or so before this trip to Fox Press, Anni had devised a second print one afternoon when we accidentally juxtaposed a negative of the first print over a Velox—a shiny proof—of it. She was happy with the resultant pattern, but did not want thin lines of blank paper to show between the shapes and the overlap, a result that was possible to achieve only through printing techniques; there could not have been a study drawing. The shop foreman, who had closely followed the development process of both prints, came over as this second image was coming off the press and asked if it wasn't even better than the concept behind the first print. Anni smiled and agreed.

As with the first image, Anni had devised the overall format and margins so that the paper size would fit into prefabricated metal-strip frames. The Alberses were both great believers in adjusting their work according to the sizes of available products. Standardization appealed. Anni had given up her loom in 1968 because she was moving to a house where no room was big enough for it; or at least this was the reason she gave. (This obfuscation through sounding deceptively matter-of-fact struck me as being on a par with her listing of her profession on her passport as "housewife." Clearly if she had wanted to keep on weaving, she could have moved to a house with enough space for her loom.) When an earnest art historian once asked Josef why he had enlarged the size of his *Homages to the Square* and had begun a group of forty-eight-by-forty-eight-inch panels, and, to Josef's irritation, suggested that it had something to do with a response to the scale of the American landscape and the oversize canvases used by the Abstract Expressionists, Josef replied that it was because he had gotten a larger station wagon.

Meanwhile, the press had been set up to print the black of the second image. As we admired the adjustments the pressman made when he switched from the proof paper to the thick and luxuriant Rives BFK that Anni had specified, the print flew off the press, its ink coverage lush and gorgeous. Just like that, one hundred and fifty sheets. It was time for lunch.

On the car ride to a local restaurant, I was again struck by how this elderly woman, for all of the visibility of her struggles, had something about her of an eager child. Her face undisguisedly revealed the battles of her youth; the rebellion against her mother and anger toward her as she rejected the trappings of upper-class existence for the rigors of Modernism; the flight from Nazism and, more arduous yet, the painful efforts a few years later to get family and friends to America when refugee ships were being turned away from our shores; the ups and downs of a marriage to a powerful and all too self-satisfied man, whose draw for other women caused no little grief for his very self-conscious wife.

Anni often said that wherever she was she felt like "the youngest person in the room." She first mentioned this to me when describing being taken, as a child, to the *Secession* show in Berlin. Her father regularly took her to museums on Sundays; this time he had opted for something more adventurous than usual. She said that as she observed the shocked crowds shaking their heads disapprovingly at the avant-garde images, she "simply thought, 'Why not?'" Telling me this when she was seventy-six, she remarked that having been the only child at that *Secession* exhibition, she had felt like the youngest person in most situations ever since, and that she still always asked, "'Why not?'"

Indeed, in attitude and interest she was younger, and fresher, than most of my contemporaries, even if I was fifty years her junior. She was like the awkward sort of adolescent girl, not the very pretty one patently pleased with herself, but rather the one who has to make the extra effort, the one intensely asking questions and looking at the world before her.

I have, since that time, heard Anni called—by a perfectly guileless woman who knew her for years at Black Mountain—"the homeliest woman who ever lived." I have also heard scores of witnesses who visited her house or saw her in public describe her as incredibly beautiful. Her face was sharply delineated, intense, and sometimes a bit crazed—like Virginia Woolf's—but her looks were quite unlike anyone else's.

Anni herself hated her features, which for her were very caught up with her Jewishness. It was uncertain to me as to whether she had a problem with being Jewish because it was associated in her mind with the facial characteristics she did not like in herself, or whether she disliked her face because to her it represented her Jewishness, which she eschewed for other reasons—but in any event, much as I would rather not acknowledge this, she was supremely uncomfortable not just with her own face and body, but also with her religious heritage and, on some levels, with her femininity. Nothing was easy for this complex person, who paradoxically was so like a true ingenue.

In the car that day, on the way to the restaurant, she was happier than usual and eagerly took the conversation from topic to topic. She and Josef led a life of remarkable solitude. Their house was truly a machine for working, with living as a secondary concern; they virtually never spent their evenings with other people, and any encounters they had were almost always for the purpose of making or showing art. Josef was not much inclined under any circumstances to discuss politics or world affairs. Anni, on the other hand, was keenly aware of the news, which came to her through a large radio and a TV that sat on rolling tables near her bed, and if her husband, she told me, felt as if the news was "all the same, always repeating itself, not as interesting as art," the events of the world fascinated her. Like Josef, she too had art as a credo; she would point out that while science constantly changes and new discoveries outdate old ideas, art offers unique stability, citing the example of a two-thousand-year-old Korean teapot with timeless appeal that affects the beholder in much the same way as the art of our own times. Nevertheless, the news mattered to her. On the way to lunch and at the restaurant, what was on her mind was a recent shooting on an Israeli airplane; most often, though, in that time period she was preoccupied with Watergate and desperate to discuss Maureen Dean or Martha Mitchell or Nixon himself. In some ways, she seemed to be a broader intellectual, and a fuller person, than Josef.

With the Israeli shooting as her topic, Anni's ambivalence about being Jewish was again apparent. Although she would subsequently change it, in her will at that time she had left her collection of Pre-Columbian textiles to the Israel Museum in Jerusalem; even though she had never been there, she felt an affinity for that country. Yet she would often describe herself as Jewish only "in the Hitler sense": her mother's family, named Ullstein, had gone through a mass family conversion to Christianity at the end of the nineteenth century, and her father, Siegfried Fleischmann, had seen to her being confirmed as a Lutheran in her childhood—in Berlin's great and fashionable Kaiser Wilhelm Gedächtniskirche. She was proud that this latter fact had enabled her and Josef to acquire the grave plots they wanted in Orange, in the section of the cemetery where Catholics like Josef were generally not allowed to be buried. (The choice of burial site was extremely important to them, in part because they wanted to be right next to the narrow driveway that wandered through the cemetery so that, once the first of them had died, the remaining one could go to the post office and then drive into the graveyard, stop the car, roll down the window, and read the mail in the company of the other—without having to get out of the car. Indeed, Anni often made such visits, although, contrary to plan, she was driven there by my wife or me, and never seemed to understand that, if she was to be right next to Josef, this meant entering from the opposite direction than they had originally

169. Josef and Anni Albers's graves, Orange Town Cemetery, Orange, Connecticut.

planned, since now she was in the passenger's seat, on the other side of the car.) But in the face of anti-Semitism, as reflected in the violence in Israel, Anni considered herself to be Jewish.

Anni had told me a month earlier about how offended she was when, at the Bauhaus, Mies van der Rohe and another architect, named Ludwig Hildesheimer, had spoken nastily of "Jewish girls from Frankfurt"; Anni said that they should have known better than to say that in front of her. I doubt that she saw any irony in this, even though she had explained to me numerous times that she didn't really consider herself to be Jewish.

But her attitude toward her own background was as unique as everything else about her. Instead of reacting with anger or fear when her Jewish heritage had forced them out of Germany, she told me she had felt "uncomfortable and responsible for Josef's having to leave his homeland after forty-five years." She considered herself "almost a weight around Josef's neck." When their boat had docked in New York, hours late because of a storm, and the photographers, there to cover the arrival of first-class passengers but then told that a famous artist was also on board, had begun to take pictures of the Modernist who had arrived to teach at Black Mountain, a jaunty newspaperman had lightened her mood considerably with a remark that might have infuriated someone else: "The wife. Let's get the wife too!" he had exclaimed. Anni quoted this to me with delight on numerous occasions. She relished his informality, and she had been happy to see someone break ranks from the crowd of reporters surrounding Josef. The attention had somehow helped assuage her guilt. There was never an iota of resentment in her retelling of the incident.

In spite of her not having been offended when others might have been, Anni often considered herself the victim of an insult or rudeness; many times her memories of people revolved around a nasty remark they had made to her. Mies, Anni would recall in another of our conversations, was central to yet another social slight for her. She and Josef were newly-weds and had just moved into one of the masters' houses at the Dessau Bauhaus. Josef told his new bride that Mies and his mistress, Lilly Reich, would be coming for dinner. Anni was determined to do her best in every way possible. Her mother had given her a butter curler, and she made a neat mound of butter balls that she put on the table prior to their guests' arrival. Mies and Reich had only just walked in when Reich looked before her and burst out, "Butter balls! Here at the Bauhaus! I should think at the Bauhaus you'd have a good solid *block* of butter."

Anni's face betrayed the wound she had incurred at the remark; she said that she had barely been able to get through dinner. Yet—perhaps as a natural consequence—this beleaguered victim could dish out much of the same. Once, a year or so following my marriage (a few months after Josef's death), my wife purchased a new dress for the opening of an exhibition of Josef's work at the Yale Art Gallery. Katharine—whose natural, no-makeup prettiness was a source of envy for Anni—was not particularly confident about clothing matters. We went together to Anni's house to pick her up before the event. Katharine was in high spirits, and, in spite of an almost total lack of vanity, felt rather pleased about the simply cut and very becoming dress. She entered Anni's bedroom—Anni, characteristically, was stretching out at the last minute to rest up before the event—with more than the usual lilt to her walk.

"Is that a new dress?" Anni asked as she gazed seriously.

"Yes," Katharine answered.

"Can you still return it?" This second question was accompanied by a sadistic smile. What the incident really revealed about Anni—

170. Josef and Anni Albers arriving in New York on board the SS Europa, November 24, 1933.

139

171. *For Kathy's Nov. 12, 1982,*
1982. Yellow marker on wove paper,
14.6 × 15.9 cm (5 ¼ × 6 ¼ inches).
Collection of Katharine Weber.

Like a medieval map of some distant island,
Anni's drawing for my twenty-seventh
birthday in 1982 signifies the uncharted
and unchartable nature of her own emotional geography. For me, the drawing has
always represented something unspoken
that existed between us. Our relationship
was one of mutual respect, cautious
affection, and occasional adversarial
sparring. The same week she made this
drawing, Anni learned that we were
expecting our second child—another rival,
perhaps, but also another member of
her not quite family.

The organic shape in the drawing
looks both flat and dimensional, because
her thick line seems to float yet it also has
an edge. The three squared dots on the
left are elements that might travel up
over the open top of the form and move
about inside. Is it a maze? Is it a living
body? Is it leaping across the page or is it
suspended, a weighted, chunky form that
her shaky pen has carved in the paper?

Did she anticipate that our second
baby would take us farther away from her?
Does the drawing depict her conception
of the three little Webers nearly devoured
by the grasping, looming form of her
distorted body? Or were we like a tiny
archipelago along her coast, sheltered in
her safe harbor?

Katharine Weber

her jealousy, her extreme mixture of kindness and nastiness, or her cruelty,
whether deliberate or inadvertent—is hard to gauge, but it was typical.

Yet in spite of this exchange, and other comparable slights,
Katharine had considerable fondness and respect for Anni—and relished
the unique workings of her mind. Once, when going to the local market
to pick up some groceries for Anni, she was making a list when Anni
requested "a banana"—pronounced bah-*nah*-nah—or, with the *a*'s similarly stretched "an avocado." No one else, Katharine felt, could want one
or the other as if they were comparable. But for Anni texture, not taste,
was the issue.

Katharine also took particular delight in Anni's obsession with
plastic. She was fascinated by the way that, when the three of us went
to the warehouse where Josef's art was stored, Anni would covet the
enormous clear bags used to cover sofas—just as she relished the sleeves
given by banks for savings-account passbooks. Katharine has often
remarked that Anni was the only person she has known who made slip-
covers for her washer and dryer. The great textile artist stitched these
herself out of shower-curtain material—which, Katharine felt, was Anni's
favorite of all substances.

At lunch on the day of our Fox Press outing, Anni also sang the praise
of Fred Harris—then a potential presidential candidate—and said that she
admired his Indian wife. I would learn over the years that many of her
political views were based on the impressions people made, on their faces
and the appearance of their character, more than on any deeper knowledge
of their platforms. Looks were paramount, in people outside the realm of
politics as well. So she and Josef liked Nelson Rockefeller, who seemed
pleasant, and had little use for Gerald Ford, "who had a face like a knee."
The novelist Robert Penn Warren was of no interest to them—because of
something about his face. It was as if people were like constructed works
of art: the qualities of balance or aggressiveness, of correctness or ugliness,
could be apprised even with a cursory view.

Anni also didn't seem to have any awareness of, or at least concern
for, the effects of her words. So she would often say, when justifying her
theory that what seems bad at first can in the long run be beneficial, "After
all, this Hitler business turned out rather well for Josef and me." She did
not grasp, even when my wife pointed it out to her, that this statement
might offend some people. Now, at lunch, Anni put forward the view that
Red China seemed the ideal country, for it had the discipline our own
society lacked. She complained that we had too much freedom at that
moment—just as there had been too much freedom at Black Mountain.
But if her effect on her audience didn't count, it seemed that her husband
was her conscience or superego: smiling apologetically, she said, "I'm glad
Josef can't hear me now. He'd be furious if he heard me say that."

When Anni and my father and I drove back to Fox Press after
lunch, I offered up the idea that I did not think any government could
improve our society, that our whole way of thinking was what needed to
change. My father asked if I thought that religion could help; I said no,
but I thought that education might. Anni was quiet throughout this dia-
logue, apparently deep in thought. Suddenly she burst out, "Through art!"

It was the faith of the Bauhaus come alive: through buildings,
through teacups, through the design of newspapers, there could result a
yes to the soul. Hard work, clarity, and brilliant art could together change
the world.

The magnificence of this woman became clear to me. She had a faith—a belief system both for herself and for society at large—to which she devoted her life. Part of the way that she served this higher purpose was by doing everything she could to support and aid Josef; he might, in ways, irritate her as a husband—the disappointments and frustrations of their relationship were sometimes all too apparent—but he was a true practitioner of the philosophy and code she revered, and to make his complex life run more smoothly, whether in the organization of an exhibition on the other side of the ocean or the doing of his laundry, served Anni's credo. But beyond that, entirely in her own right, she was daring and giving—and constantly looking. Josef had declared, shortly after arriving at Black Mountain, that his goal was "to make open the eyes"—which soon became "to open eyes," the words synonymous with his highly influential teaching—and no one exemplified this better than his uncompromising, sometimes obstreperous, wife. Anni and Josef together—for all the yin and yang of their two sometimes contrasting personalities—had a common raison d'être. They believed that art could change the world as nothing else could. Morality, balance, decency, a responsiveness to the richness of the universe and of human life: all of this could be revealed and abetted through paint, thread, and ink.

Anni was immensely serious in all this, but she was also wry. When, a few weeks later, we took up the topic of social change again, she recalled that my father had offered that improvement might be made "through sex." She repeated this with a glimmer. Sex, I would later learn, was one of her favorite topics. She had to know someone very well before bringing it up, but, sometimes playful, sometimes mischievous, she had lots of questions she wanted answered, lots of words she had heard on television and needed to have explained. Once, when a student at Black Mountain asked her who in history she would most like to have been or who her favorite imaginary persona was, Anni, with her rather sticklike figure and nunlike persona, did not miss a beat in her answer: "Mae West."

Back at Fox Press after lunch, Anni again bore the look of glee—of profound contentment—with which she commenced any activity having to do with the making of art. Once she had gone through the diplomatic niceties with the pressmen, she seated herself again on the simple wooden chair—bearing an uncanny resemblance to Balthus's portrait of the Vicomtesse de Noailles, in which that great patron of the avant-garde was painted not in one of her elaborate residences but rather, dressed austerely, on a simple side chair in the artist's rugged atelier, her face serious, her thoughts turned inward. Anni became both resolute and concentrated, a missionary on a campaign, a research scientist peering into a microscope in the hope that what would soon be visible might provide an answer to an unsolved mystery of existence. She approved the tone and color mix of the red for her first print, and off it rolled. Then, watching the press wash-up, Anni compared this necessity to the counting of threads in weaving. It was all part of the process of art, she remarked. The emotional security, the sense of hope, the sublime feeling of possibility afforded by that process were her elixir.

Now it was time to run the brown of her second print. Josef had selected the precise ink a few days earlier from the PMS ink swatch book. In that simple act of collaboration, one could see the answer to the often-asked questions about their relationship as fellow artists, as a husband and wife achieving different levels of success in similar fields, as a man and woman living and working together in the twentieth century. The Alberses

172. Anni Albers in her kitchen at 8 North Forest Circle, New Haven, Connecticut, 1958.

were like a two-person religious sect. Their goal was simple: to make the best possible art. They cared above all about honesty in their approach to this task. Like two builders working side by side on the erection of the same edifice, occasionally they might take advice from one another, hear a helpful suggestion; otherwise, in their work, they mainly just kept their eyes on the job, not on each other.

One hears stories that suggest that there was competitiveness in their relationship, like that of Josef leaving the house when the director of the Yale Art Gallery arrived there to buy one of Anni's weavings for the museum and not returning until after the deal was complete. But was this out of jealousy, his not being able to bear his wife's success, as the observer inferred? Or was it because he was then at the peak of his fame, particularly in the Yale community following the publication of his *Interaction of Color*, and he did not want to steal the stage but rather to let his wife enjoy the attention? The common claim is that Anni suffered as the lesser-known of two great artists. On the other hand, there are weavers who bitterly maintain that as Mrs. Josef Albers she had entrée where they did not, that she benefited considerably from the visits to her house of art-world luminaries, and from a last name that was known by every critic and museum director. Did her work amount to less because she functioned, to use her favorite term, as "that dragon at the door," protecting her husband from the sometimes unwelcome advances of journalists, gallerists, and students? Did she lose out because of the time she spent doing his laundry or preparing his meals?

Indeed, Josef was so inept in this latter process that once, when Anni was heading to the hospital for a scheduled operation that would require her absence of three days, she left out a row of cans of food, instructed him (twice) on how to use the electric can opener, and showed him precisely what was involved in turning the stove on and off. But, as she often pointed out, the activity of thinking about food and cooking it only entered her life once she was fifty; in her childhood she had lived in the sort of household where only staff entered the kitchen; at the Bauhaus there had been a cafeteria, at Black Mountain a dining room. Only in 1950, when she and Josef arrived in New Haven, did Anni have to think about making dinner. And rather than resenting the task, she approached it like a new artistic medium. Josef, after all, used the word "recipe" to refer to the color arrangements of his *Homages*; Anni too saw cooking as an act of taking components and combining them effectively, even if it was an area where she favored minimal expenditure of time and energy and aimed merely for adequate, not exciting, results. (When I was first setting up modest bachelor digs and clearly had little idea about how to cook, she advised me on her favorite recipe, for "*himmel und erde*"—heaven and earth. It consisted of taking a jar of applesauce and mixing it, in equal parts, with instant mashed potatoes.)

But whatever the details, Anni often claimed that she liked doing things for Josef. When he died, one of her immediate laments was that she would miss the need to buy him shirts and socks. On quite a different level, she once told me of an occasion when she was pleased that her husband asked for her help when he wanted to end a love affair and could not manage to shake off the woman on his own; Anni, in complete collaboration with Josef, met the forlorn mistress in order to stop the relationship once and for all. The terms of their marriage are hardly to everyone's taste, but apparently they suited the participants.

Anni's memory of their early courtship reveals a singular lack of confidence, which may explain a lot of her subsequent attitudes. At her first Bauhaus Christmas party—in Weimar in 1922—she wore a dress of brilliant green silk accented by a little pink velvet ribbon. Santa Claus had many gifts to distribute from his huge basket; Anni—by her own description, "a shy newcomer"—knew that she would not get one. Suddenly Santa called out her name. He handed her a print of Giotto's *Flight into Egypt*. The card was addressed to her from Josef; the thrill was unequivocal.

173. Giotto, *Flight into Egypt*, 1304–06. Scrovegni Chapel, Padua.

The following June, when she was home in Berlin for her twenty-third birthday, Anni was similarly surprised when a package arrived containing a twelve-inch-high bronze copy of a lithe and graceful Egyptian figure at the Pergamon Museum. Only two copies of the figure existed, and the near-penniless Josef had secured this one for her. It was an image I knew well, since Anni still had it at her bedside when I knew her, on the plain white wooden bookshelf only a few feet from her pillow. In fact, every photograph of anywhere she ever lived shows the bronze next to her bed.

Anni told me that shortly after receiving the Egyptian figure, she earned some money by selling necklaces that she made out of little beads, and this enabled her to take Josef, whom she was now seeing often, "to a good tailor to have a conventional suit made." His usual garb was a khaki corduroy jacket with a hint of white silk scarf showing beneath it; while Anni considered this very becoming, she was also concerned about its unconventionality. She reacted similarly to the way he wore his hair forward in bangs: "I still fall for any man with this haircut today," she allowed with a smile, but she added that he had to change this haircut for the reason that "the waiters in Weimar restaurants were inattentive because of his bohemian looks." In a similar vein, Anni felt he should have the new suit as a necessary prelude to a visit to the world of her parents; she wanted them to feel easy about the young man from "the adventurous art school." These attitudes—both the aesthetic preferences and the notions about clothing in its sociological context, or visual style and the message of class—were with Anni throughout her life.

Indeed, the entire Fleischmann family was charmed by Josef in his suit. Anni's brother, ten years younger than she, "could not leave Josef's side." Her younger sister wrote to Anni at the Bauhaus just to thank her for bringing home "the beautiful Memling." Her mother would later tell Josef that if he ever had any real trouble with Anni, the house was always open to him without her. When Josef, in 1925, was the first student to be asked by Gropius to become a master at the Bauhaus, meaning to Anni (so surprisingly traditional in certain ways) that she could now ask her parents about their getting married, her parents gave their full support; the wealthy Jewish Berliners readily embraced the impoverished Westfalian Catholic, even if Josef's father and stepmother, back in Bottrop, were far less comfortable with the match. Anni and Josef were wed in a Catholic church a short walk from the Fleischmanns' apartment—with only her immediate family present as guests—and then repaired to the elegant Hotel Adlon for a celebration lunch. Larger parties and events, Anni and Josef felt, were not for them. They belonged, rather, "to those who do things like that"; all of the Alberses' time and energy had to be focused on the making of art.

174 and 175. Reproduction Egyptian figurine given to Anni by Josef on her twenty-third birthday (above), and the figurine on Anni's bedside shelf at 808 Birchwood Drive, Orange, Connecticut, 1994 (below).

In 1953 and 1954, when Josef was teaching in Ulm while Anni remained in New Haven, they wrote to each other all the time—thus leaving correspondence that is one of the few written testimonials of their particular communication with one another.

An emphasis on clothing, as well as Anni's delight in helping Josef, are recurring themes. She wrote to him shortly after his departure, in a letter full of chat about the details of life—dinners out with friends and family (they were apparently more sociable during this period than at the time I knew them) and Anni's usual mix of pleasure and fear of things done or said wrong, "I started painting your ceiling now, all the paper is off. It goes slow. But all your shirts have their new collars. So at least something gets done."[5] Pleasure, rather than resentment, is a salient quality, as is her love for her husband and for the sights and miracles of existence they savored together:

> *The moss outside looks wonderful, greener and greener as the days get wetter.*
> *Almost 2 weeks gone by !!! two weeks less.*
> *Now I'll go and paint some more ceiling, being in your room helps.*

Four days later, after writing to him almost daily with typewritten pages full of news, she concluded,

> *I like best being in your room.*
> *How is the dark beer?*
> *love and love   Ank.*

Three days after that, there was more of the same:

> *Still painting your room, the area with the 2 doors now has two coats and tomorrow I hope to get the last one so that that is done. Remains still the niche toward the street . . . and the radiator.*
> *But it begins to look wonderful.*

Ironies abound here. Josef's father had been a housepainter, while Anni's had been someone who hired workmen for such tasks. Josef made his art with paint—the medium that Anni would gladly have opted for over textiles—which she only used now, in this menial way, to redo his room in his absence. But no such factors or resentment entered her conscious thoughts. Her delight was total. Two-and-a-half weeks later, she reported,

> *I finished your room today, the awful radiator is now fine white with two coats of enamel, and now it can smell itself out until you come back. As a special treat, I made up your bed today, a little early, but it made me feel good.*

Along with news of arrangements with the Sidney Janis Gallery in New York made on Josef's behalf, with a keen response to his letters (or their lack), with chat about further evenings out and details of bank statements and other aspects of domestic life, this woman, who was so ambivalent about her own appearance, so seemingly plain while at the same time intensely self-conscious, also reported, at the end of one letter, "And most important: a new hairdresser who is supposed to cut excellently, will go there Monday!!!" The report came five days later:

> *Most important: that I have a hairdresser who has a sense of form!!! Has taken drawing lessons from one of your students, Slutsky or so, and he wants to continue with someone again, perhaps Si. I think you would agree that it is much better already and gradually he will get my hair into better shape when all that was cut wrongly has grown back.*

How Robert Slutsky and Si Sillman—two of Josef's most successful students at Yale—would have felt knowing that the element of their sense of form that mattered most to their teacher's wife had to do with her coif is questionable.

Yet Anni was not being frivolous; hair was a serious matter. In evaluating Josef's students, if Anni wanted to denigrate any of them, all that she had to do was refer to "the bearded ones."

Nov. 28.53

Juwe,

Die Überfahrt klingt nicht so besonders erholend! I only
hope you were not too miserable and that you recovered on
the rest of the trip. The menu looks enormous!

And by now I hope you are in Ulm and that it is what you
had hoped for. Sofar I had a letter from Southhampton. Maybe
another one will come today.

All goes well here and people are nice. Thanksgiving I was
next door at the Hall's, with your photos, and all was really
nice. One afternoon the Chaets came with the archaeology
girl and that was nice too. One evening I had Si and Jim and
Sheilagh and she is going to take her jeep station wagon to
New York with Si and me to pick up the Cooper Union things.
I had offered to pay for all expenses involved. So that will
be Dec. 1. if there is not snow by then, as the weatherman
has announced för these days. Today Wu has asked Hans & Betty
including children (!) and me for dinner. I am embarrassed
that by bringing the children he will have such a crowd. I
asked him to bring them first for cocktails here. They come
already early in the afternoon and Wu is taking them through
the gallery.

Paps writes he plans to stay till april. What then, I don't
know, Hans writes he wants to take up the money problem.

Yesterday Si took me after lunch with them,to the upper part
of the Gallery with the Asia things etc. Looks really fine.

George Howe I have not reached yet. Never there. Do write
him a postcard. I'll also try again. *Also Si, maybe.*

A nice note from Farnsworth, Chicago.

And one from Bobby... I'll go there for Christmas.

I started painting your ceiling now, all the paper is off.
It goes slow. But all your shirts have their new collars.
So at least something gets done.

The moss outside looks wonderful, greener and greener as
the days get wetter.

Almost 2 weeks gone by!!!   two weeks less.

Now I'll go and paint some more ceiling, being in your room
helps.

so love,

Deine Änki.

176. Letter from Anni Albers to Josef Albers,
November 28, 1953.

145

177. Anni and Josef Albers with Maude
Gröte, Nuremberg, November 1968.

Josef returned for a second stint in Ulm in the spring of 1955, so again there are letters that document both the feelings and the details that mattered to the Alberses. Anni's voice reveals the same reserved exuberance that is evident in her art, a comparable immersion in tactile and visual pleasures, and a need for emotional connection that is as strong as the feeling for linkages of thread and shape. In a letter written to "Juvel" on May 12, she assured him, "Here all is fine and I am not lonely because I have such a good feeling about us and the 17. to look forward to. Aug. 17 is what they say here is the arrival date." She also reported,

> *When you left, took taxi to Abercrombie and Fitch and bought*
> *myself a really good coat, reversible, tweed and rain-coat, inside-out-*
> *side, think you will approve, expensive too, 73,77. In other stores*
> *saw nothing that looked right. So now I have a good one too.*

They were still both wearing these coats when I knew them more than fifteen years later; in a way the Alberses sometimes looked like brother and sister as much as they did husband and wife, and the simple, generous cut of these coats with raglan sleeves gave them a comparable look of timeless fashion. The warm tweed and practical waterproof material were a stylish and appealing combination.

Art and other aspects of the visual world permeate this correspondence. Anni reported to Josef, of a show at the Museum of Modern Art, "There is a french painter in there, Manessier, whom I like. Pictures look fine, he looks right and what he writes is beautiful, I think." At the same time, the letters show an equal concern for the functional. Shortly before going to teach at the Haystack School in Maine, Anni informed Josef,

> *Bought myself some light colored and washable cotton slacks for*
> *Maine. Of all places it was finally Sears Roebuck where I found*
> *some decent ones. Tried Abercrombie etc. . . . And there too,*
> *I bought myself a birthday present, a little gray metal typewriter*
> *table on rollers, charming, only 7.50 amazingly enough. It comes*
> *packed in parts and on the 12th [June 12, her birthday] I will*
> *get it out and put it together, think you will like it and it seems*
> *just right to roll around on my own. At least that's what I think/*
> *Hope it will work out when its set up.*
> *so love and love, from Änkele*

And six days later, on the twelfth, this woman, who so relished the assembling of components, wrote to "Juvel" first that she had received three birthday letters from him on time—"so it really turned into a fine birthday with your powerful help"—and added,

> *And now I am sitting at my new little gray metal typewriter-table,*
> *which rolls around the room,—I had saved it for today, the putting*
> *together of the parts and it took me a good part of the morning*
> *and was interesting to do.*

After Josef's death, Anni found it easy to fault him; in her memories he was indifferent at times to her bad health, competitive ("He told me my first prints looked 'like wallpaper'"), and secretive—particularly about the financial well-being that came to him late in life. At the same time, she saw herself as equally difficult ("When he made his first squares, I said, 'They're like Easter eggs. If that's all you paint, now we'll never have enough to eat.'"). But at least in the way that I often saw them in the last years of their life together, through their fiftieth wedding anniversary less than a year before Josef died in 1976, and as their great Black Mountain companions and housemates Ted and Bobbie Dreier knew them to be, the Alberses, in spite of the occasional squabble, were mutually supportive teammates, intensely respectful of each other's dedication to art,

146

seriousness of purpose, integrity, and achievement. Josef always wrote the titles and other information on the back of Anni's weavings because his handwriting was neater than hers. In some cases, he also suggested a color for her to use. Likewise, Anni voiced a preference for certain of Josef's *Homages*. In fact, in spite of her initial response, she ultimately found them glorious, so much so that after Josef's death we discovered that, in addition to the thousands of artworks he had already left her, he had, on the backs of those over which she had voiced particular enthusiasm and on others that he considered his ultimate achievements, written "N.F.S."—not for sale—"Property of A.A." So within Josef's collection there was a collection that came to her as a complete surprise in her period of deepest mourning. He had also—but this she always knew—given her the first of every print edition.

Anni was proud that Josef had selected the brown for the second print she made at Fox Press. He was, after all, the colorist. It helped, of course, that for years they were in different fields within the same arena—she was the weaver, while he pursued glass and metal and wood and then paint—but even when both were printmakers the nature of their work was so different (he was mainly involved, in the late stage of his graphics, the point at which Anni took up the medium, in color as the central issue, she more in line and surface and the particularities of the process) that competition was not a factor. Rather, they went side by side to the work-shop of Ken Tyler, where they made many of their prints, taking turns and offering suggestions. They knew better than to try to work together on an artwork—both were too strong-willed, and too potentially cantan-kerous, for that—but they completely supported and respected each other's work and the priority of it in their lives. (Other interests—social, family, recreational—all were relegated to a secondary sphere.)

Following Josef's death—she outlived him by nearly two decades—Anni often recalled the ways in which she had helped him; she was immensely pleased to have done so. For one thing, she would say with pride, with a slightly arrogant and superior look on her face, "I had to teach him manners." She, after all, came from a world where people served her; he did not. She could guide the son of a Westfalian laborer on how to behave in the fancy houses of art collectors. Then there was her knowledge of English, which made such a difference—Josef knew none—when they emigrated to America in 1933. This, too, reflected the class difference of their backgrounds. Anni had had an Irish nurse and governess. So she could teach him English, and also interpret for him. At Black Mountain, when a woman named Emily Zastrow functioned as an inter-preter for Josef's teaching, Anni sat in on his class one day. Mrs. Zastrow made him sound too Teutonic, Anni felt: "If he said, 'Do have a look at this and see what you think,' she would say, 'And he insists that you think about it!'" Anni demanded that Mrs. Zastrow relinquish the job and that Josef do his best on his own, in English.

Anni recounted a telling anecdote about Mrs. Zastrow and Josef and herself. Mrs. Zastrow's son was a German government official. His doting mother regularly left pro-Nazi clippings all around the Lee Hall living room, the main place where people congregated at Black Mountain. "I, of course, picked them up and threw them in the fireplace," Anni told me, "while my honest and very careful Josef insisted, 'You have no right to do this; they aren't yours.' So how did he go about it? He picked them up and put them into the back pages of the newspapers, which were thrown away every morning."

She also told a story at her own expense about teaching English to Josef. Once they were walking in a field near Black Mountain when Josef saw a sign for "Brown's pasture," and inquired, "Was ist das, Ankë: pasture?" Her answer was certain: "Oh that's very clear, Juppi, it's the opposite of future."

Humor was one of Anni's salient traits, and it was often very dark. Once, when my wife was visiting her in the hospital, when Anni was recovering from a broken hip, and it seemed that the patient might go home the next day, Katharine said, "So, if I come tomorrow and you're not here . . ." Anni interrupted her with the instruction, "Send a wreath." When an exhibition of her work opened in 1985 at the Renwick Gallery in Washington, D.C., and a well-meaning visitor, who had come from New Haven just for the occasion, proudly presented her with a stiff and overarranged bouquet of flowers, the presenter's face aglow with pleasure, Anni, in a wheelchair, put them on her lap with the words, "For my casket." The woman stopped in her tracks. I am not sure if Anni even thought to let her off the hook with a simple thank you; she did not mind making people outside her chosen circle uncomfortable.

In this respect, I once failed at all diplomatic efforts to get Anni to receive an extremely thoughtful and courteous curator from the Museum of Modern Art because she was in a bad mood that day— a combination of a digestive disorder and a phone call not having come in from a friend from whom she was eager to hear. She had no trouble being truly nasty to this amiable museum professional, who had made the journey just to see her, loved her work, and, additionally, would help her in the world. It is no wonder then that Philip Johnson, the central figure behind the Alberses' coming to America and the curator of Anni's first major museum show, at the Museum of Modern Art in 1949, told me that he had realized early on that Anni was not someone who would act in her own best interests, that she had no instinct for public relations. It was almost as if she associated gentility with fraudulence, good PR with the sort of artistic shilly-shallying that infuriated her in people like Johnson himself—someone both she and Josef considered a traitor to their artistic credo and to the Modernism he had once embraced through their friend and associate Mies van der Rohe. Alas, there was a side of Anni that was simply perverse—and not very nice.

But when happy, Anni could be an angel. Back at Fox Press, there was trouble with the line-up of the brown in the second print in juxtaposition with the black. A long, tense hour followed. Proof after proof came through without the desired effect. I paced back and forth restlessly. Anni sat patiently. As she reviewed each sheet, she simply made further suggestions to the stripper and pressman, nodding her head "no" or smiling "yes" at their latest adjustments. Her object was to avoid white hairlines between shapes. What I knew was that there was something about this image, both in its systematization and lack of simple resolution, that was to resemble, or at least simulate, both the structure of gems and the nature of plant growth as elucidated by Goethe in his *Metamorphosis of Plants*. Gems, Anni pointed out, depended on irregularity in their cellular structure in order to be strong. Plant growth, according to the passages she cherished in Goethe, revealed a repetition of number systems; if there were three parts to the roots, there were also three parts to the stems and leaves. She had evoked both of these qualities in her initial design. But now she had to resolve the hairline problem; having achieved her well-thought-out design, she wanted to refine it according to the dictates of her

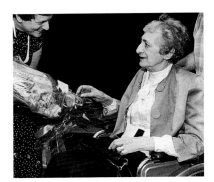

178. Anni Albers at the opening of an exhibition of her work, the Renwick Gallery of the National Museum of American Art, Smithsonian Institution, Washington, D.C., June 12, 1985.

ever-demanding eye. There must also be a clarity and serenity as powerful as the playfulness and mystery inherent in this complex pattern achieved through printerly overlapping. The tools of the process were essential to the creation of the artwork, and now they had to be manipulated in compliance with the artist's eye. It was a result that could be realized only by working in tandem, and no one could have been more respectful of the technicians involved in the process. Without condescension, she treated them not merely as coworkers but rather as heroes.

We watched the pressman use his wrench to change the register a hair one way, then the other. Lining up some sections of the image to avoid the white gaps in various places created wider gaps in others. We tried blowing up one pattern with the camera—here the stripper participated—but this destroyed the whole. I kept pacing. Finally the foreman suggested using the Rives BFK paper saved for the final prints; its thickness would make a difference because the flimsy trial paper was expanding. For Anni, it was like the working of thick and thin fibers, of jute with cellophane: a world of texture and reality she well knew. To conserve the remaining Rives, we first ran the brown on some discards from the first print. Anni found that the red and brown together—this proofing of the second print on top of the discards from the first—looked so architectural that she took samples to show architects as possible patterns for tiled walls. And fortunately the heavier paper made the difference. Once the pressman had touched up the plate by hand while it was on the roller, thus getting rid of the few white lines that remained—with the artist's profound admiration and delight—she approved the line-up at last. He ran the print, and we were done.

At lunch, Anni had praised the Italian bread, explaining that "Josef, a true Westfalian, lives for bread." While we were monitoring the afternoon printing session, my father had gone out to procure a loaf, which he handed to Anni along with some scratch pads as we were heading out to the car. "I am leaving with treasures," the former master of the Bauhaus said enthusiastically; she truly meant it.

Our drive, however, made her anxious. She was a poor passenger at best—clearly in the habit of doing a lot of back-seat driving when Josef was at the wheel—and now we encountered torrential rains. These, Anni said, reminded her of Mexico, where they had gone fourteen times, initially when they were nearly penniless. Mexico had had an enormous influence on both of them; Anni said that "art was everywhere there": in people's clothing, in their beads, in the paint trim on the adobe houses, in the cheapest country pottery. It was a visual world—more, perhaps, than a verbal one. I would not normally link Anni with Antonin Artaud, but given Artaud's passion for nonverbal communication, his emphasis on gesture and facial expression rather than text, his feeling for the exotic and ear for the voice of the ancient gods, and the role of Mexico in Artaud's life when he fled Paris in the 1930s, I have come to see Anni and Josef and Artaud as sophisticated European Moderns of the same camp—even if the peyote that flavored Artaud's every thought in the Mexican villages he visited, where he might well have walked by Anni and Josef, would have been anathema to the artistic pair, who were so intent on control and rationalism.

But although Anni was happy to have the sheets of rain evoke memories of Tenayuca and Oaxaca, they alarmed her; the woman who by all accounts had been quite resolute in her flight from Nazi Germany was visibly on the edge of panic. I offered to follow the lead of a few other cars and pull over to the side of the highway until the downpour let up.

179. Josef Albers, *Paul Klee, (Guetary) Biarritz VIII '29*, 1929. Collage of three photographs, mounted on board (detail). The Josef and Anni Albers Foundation, Bethany.

180. Paul Klee, *Gifts for I* (*Gabe für I*), 1928. Tempera on gessoed canvas mounted on wood, 40 × 55.9 cm (15 ¾ × 22 inches). The Museum of Modern Art, New York, Gift of James Thrall Soby.

"Please," Anni gently implored. Under the shelter of an overpass, I turned off the motor.

Anni's face betrayed considerable relief. "You deserve a reward," she said in a tone more jocular than patronizing. "Well, I know you've been wanting to know about Paul Klee. I think I will tell you the story of his fiftieth birthday."

It was 1929. Klee, Anni told me, was her "god at the time"; he was also her next-door neighbor. Although the Swiss painter was, in her eyes, aloof and unapproachable—"like Saint Christopher carrying the weight of the world on his shoulders"—she admired him tremendously. She had even acquired one of his watercolors—the purchase having been a rare public admission of her family's wealth (she told me that she had been so embarrassed by the appearance at the Dessau Bauhaus of her uncles in a Hispano Suiza that she had begged them to leave immediately)—out of one of the exhibitions in which Klee tacked up his most recent work in a corridor of the new Bauhaus building. As her god approached his major birthday, Anni heard that three other students in the weaving workshop were hiring a small plane from the Junkers aircraft plant, not far away, so that they could have this mystical, other-worldly man's birthday presents descend to him from above; he was beyond having gifts arrive on the earthly plane.

Klee's presents were to arrive in a large package shaped like an angel. Anni made the curled hair for it out of tiny, shimmering brass shavings. Other Bauhauslers made the gifts the angel would carry: a print from Lyonel Feininger, a lamp from Marianne Brandt, some small objects from the wood workshop.

Anni was not originally scheduled to be on the small Junkers aircraft from which the angel was to descend, but when she arrived at the airfield with her three friends, the pilot deemed her so light that he invited her to get on board. For all of them, it was the first flight. As the cold October air penetrated her coat and the pilot joked with the young weavers by doing complete turnabouts as they huddled together in the open cockpit, Anni was so obsessed with abstract art that, rather than responding with fear, what struck her most was the sudden awareness of a new visual dimension. She had been living on one optical plane, and now saw from a very different vantage point.

She served the mission by spotting Klee's house next door to hers and Josef's, in the row of masters' houses a short walk from the main building. As planned, they let out the gift. It landed with a bit of a crash. But Klee was pleased nonetheless—he would memorialize the unusual presents and their delivery in a painting. Josef, however, was less impressed. Later that afternoon he asked Anni if she had seen the idiots flying around overhead. Anni smiled mischievously as she recalled this. "I told him I was one of them," she said with her usual tone of unperturbed defiance.

Although in the course of time Anni came to remember Josef as indifferent to her needs and comfort, when we pulled into the driveway of their house after completing our drive when the torrents lessened to mere rain, he opened the automatic garage door as we made the turn in order to spare his wife any unnecessary steps in the rain. He must have been waiting at the window for quite some time. The two of them were ebullient as she handed him some prints and the bread; their life together, austere and isolated as it may have been, seemed a panoply of pleasures at that moment.

They were, of course, both people for whom the idea of survival had real meaning—initially because of the struggles of the Bauhaus; then the horrible realities of Nazi Germany; after that, even once they were in safer territory, the intense financial pressure at Black Mountain and, subsequently, following Josef's unhappy departure from Yale; now the vicissitudes of old age—and Anni's safe return in the storm afforded them palpable relief. In fact, this may be one of the reasons that Anni took particular delight in aborting plans entirely because of bad weather. She once told me that breaking a date was one of life's great pleasures, comparable only to returning something to a department store. Dressed and ready to go for an outing to New York, only to have a phone call suggesting that because of inclement weather the meeting in the city be rescheduled, Anni, rather than showing disappointment, looked like someone who had been given an unexpected treat. In one of the letters she sent to Josef in Ulm, she wrote, with regard to a lecture scheduled half an hour away, "To my enormous pleasure my talk in Bridgeport was canceled because of a new snowstorm we are having." Of course there were other factors as well; two days earlier she had written to Josef, "The Bridgeport group, Weavers Guild, makes me feel bad. Everything they touch they do wrongly, even my name is spelled wrongly, Annie Alkers of N.Y.! Think I'll speak about Quality there, if I can get my thoughts straight."

The day following my trip with Anni to Fox Press, the pressman and stripper told me that it was too bad that all of our customers were not like Anni. Unlike the advertising men and purchasing agents, who said that they did not care what the machine could or could not do as long as they got what they wanted, she worked in tandem with the equipment. "The lady with the cane," the bindery foreman added, "really liked the shrink wrap too. She figured out right away how it does the corners."

  In her person she had brought into the printing plant some of the same poetry and lightness that demarcate her artwork. And in keeping with the ideals that Gropius had established at the Bauhaus, the pioneering art school he had opened in Weimar more than fifty years earlier, she had rendered nil the boundaries between craft and art. She had allowed machinery and creativity to have a common voice, and technical restraints and possibilities to be the aid, not the foe, of inspiration. The practical and the spiritual were one.

  Indeed, for the rest of her life, even after Josef and all the others had died, the last living Bauhausler kept the vision alive—as her art will do forever.

181. Anni Albers with Nicholas Fox Weber and *Fox II*, in the living room at 808 Birchwood Drive, Orange, Connecticut, 1981.

Notes

1. This translation of the sixth-century BC Chinese philosopher is quoted from a handwritten note in Anni's papers at the Josef and Anni Albers Foundation; it may be her own translation from a German source.
2. This and all subsequent statements by Anni are from conversations with the author that took place in 1974 and 1975 while the author was interviewing the artist on tape in preparation for a book devoted to her work.

3. Camilla Lyons, a pre-med student at Yale College as well as an art historian, provided this information in a memo of Nov. 19, 1998.
4. Bertrand Russell, *The Conquest of Happiness* (London: Horace Liveright, 1930), p. 118.
5. All letters are in The Josef and Anni Albers Foundation archives and are quoted as they appear.

Anni Albers
1899–1994

Pandora Tabatabai Asbaghi

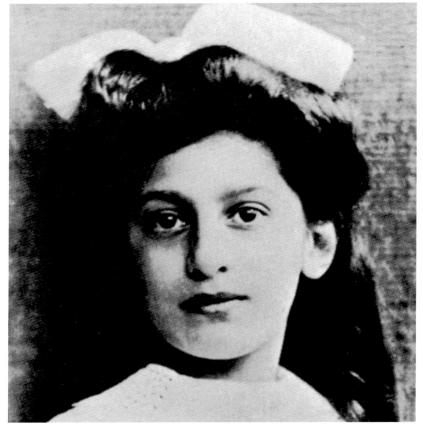

182. Anni Albers, ca. 1908.

Anni Albers left us a compact but pure legacy that comprises not only her artworks but also her writings and other statements, which, together, provide a clear guideline for thinking about design and art. An artist, designer, writer, and teacher, for most of the century she was an interested if somewhat detached observer of political, industrial, and artistic developments. Her curiosity was that of a true pioneer, and her work consistently reveals a deep respect for the universal truths of the past as well as a search for solutions only possible in the present. Connecting craft to industry, unifying art with design, generously sharing her learning with others, she made few claims about her own originality, speaking instead of rediscovery, re-invention.

Albers rarely expressed regret about the necessity of leaving Germany in 1933 for an uncertain future in the United States; rather, she preferred to dwell on the consequent opportunities that came to her and Josef. As they explored Mexico and the American Southwest, they were both deeply affected by the scale of the land-scape, by the aesthetic marvels of the indigenous art and architecture, and, in Mexico, by the beauty of the ancient culture that seemed to grow in the ground in the form of the tiny Pre-Columbian artifacts that they collected with a shared passion.

Was it Albers's physical dis-ability or the social and cultural environment of her past that never quite allowed her to move freely and express herself with complete independence? Under her elegance and modesty, and despite the sure hand and voice in her art and

her writing, there lay an ambition for greater recognition that was at odds with her reclusive nature.

Here, an account of Albers's life, arranged around the artist's words along with those of people who knew her well or who have studied her art, proves that her legacy to us stands alone and is worthy of our consideration today, not only for its historic value but also for what it can continue to teach us about the place of art in our daily lives.

1899–1921

Anni Albers was born Annelise Else Frieda Fleischmann at 5 Lessingstrasse in the Charlottenburg section of Berlin on June 12, 1899. She was the eldest of three children born to Siegfried Fleischmann (1873–1963) and Toni Ullstein Fleischmann (1877–1946). "[When she was growing up] her mother's family, the Ullsteins of publishing fame, seemed slightly commercial to her, her father's (a furniture manufacturer) more aristocratic."[1] Albers's brother, Hans Farman (born in 1909), who changed his name from Fleischmann when he moved to the United States in 1936, notes that the women of the Ullstein family were well educated, but were expected to "get married on their own . . . whereas the sons inherited the [family] fortune."[2] Hans's wife, Elizabeth (Betty), notes, "[Albers] swam against the

183. Hans Farman (Fleischmann), 1930, photographed by Josef Albers.

184. Lotte Benfey (née Fleischmann), ca. 1920.

185. Siegfried Fleischmann, 1930, photographed by Josef Albers.

186. Toni Ullstein Fleischmann, ca. 1940.

stream, she was rebellious and she resented her mother. . . . Anni had some kind of artistic longings and leanings in her. Her family, in her mind . . . didn't feel the artistic leanings as she did."[3] Around 1912 the family moved to a large apartment at 7 Meinekestrasse, near the Kurfürstendamm. Albers's sister, Lotte Benfey (1900–1987), recalled, "We had eight or nine rooms. There was the music room that was only used for parties. . . . There was a room for Anni's painting. . . . Opa [Siegfried Fleischmann] had furniture and antiques. . . . He loved to go to art museums."[4]

When Albers was an adolescent, her mother arranged for her to have an art tutor. Later, from 1916 to 1919, she studied painting with Martin Brandenburg, an Impressionist painter.

[In my] early teens. . . . I saw portraits that [Oskar] Kokoschka had drawn and I thought they were beautiful, that the character of a person came out much better than in a photograph, for instance. . . . I made a terrible [portrait] of my mother, which I took under my arms with my mother to try to get to Dresden, where Kokoschka lived, and see if he had classes where I could learn. And he had one look at that and said, "Why do you paint?" I was fifteen or sixteen so that was the smashing answer and that was the end of that.[5]

In 1920 Albers attended the Kunstgewerbeschule (school of applied arts) in Hamburg. After two months she was disappointed with the learning program and sought out other sorts of instruction.

154

1922–24

Fortunately a leaflet came my way from the Bauhaus [on which] there was a print by Feininger, a cathedral, and I thought that was very beautiful and also at that time, through some connections—somebody told me—[that it] was a new experimental place. . . . I thought, "That looks more like it," so this is what I tried.[6]

"In a rented room, with a bath available only once a week, the young Berliner who was used to a seamstress and laundress applied to the experimental school. She was rejected at first, but was admitted on her second attempt."[7]

Albers entered the mandatory Vorkurs (preliminary course) at the Bauhaus on April 21, 1922, studying with Georg Muche in the first semester and with Johannes Itten in the second.

Well the Bauhaus today is thought of always as a school, a very adventurous and interesting one, to which you went and were taught something; that it was a readymade spirit. But when I got there in 1922 that wasn't true at all. It was in a great muddle and there was a great searching going on from all sides. And people like Klee and Kandinsky weren't recognized as the great masters. They were starting to find their way. And this kind of general searching was very exciting. And . . . this is what I called the "creative vacuum."[8]

The Bauhaus leaflet that attracted Albers to Weimar had been written by Walter Gropius, the founder of this new school of art and design. It stated that "any person of good repute, without regard to age or sex, whose previous education is deemed adequate by the Council of Masters, will be admitted, as far as space permits."[9]

187. Anni Albers, ca. 1923, photographed by Lucia Moholy-Nagy.

188. Georg Muche and members of the weaving workshop at the Bauhaus, Weimar, ca. 1923. Anni Albers is at the extreme right.

But despite the school's apparent commitment to gender equality, Gropius wrote to a woman who applied for admission in 1920, "It is not advisable, in our experience, that women work in the heavy craft areas such as carpentry and so forth. For this reason a women's section has been formed at the Bauhaus which works particularly with textiles; bookbinding and pottery also accept women. We are fundamentally opposed to the education of women as architects."[10]

The entering students had to enter a workshop and the workshops I thought I might try all weren't quite suited for me. For instance, I didn't want wall painting because I didn't like climbing on ladders and I didn't want metal workshop because it is so hard and pointed. I didn't want woodworking where you had to lift heavy beams, and there was one left that was a glass

workshop and there was already somebody in there [Josef Albers] with whom I would have loved to be in that workshop but they didn't allow a second person because there was not chance of any kind of further work there.[11]

So after completing the Vorkurs, Albers reluctantly entered the weaving workshop in 1923.

My beginning was far from what I had hoped for: fate put into my hands limp threads! Threads to build a future? But distrust turned into belief and I was on my way.[12]

Albers credited Gunta Stölzl for most of her early training, claiming that she had "almost an animal feeling for textiles."

I learned from Gunta, who was a great teacher. We sat down and tried to do it. Sometimes we sat together and tried to solve problems of construction.[13]

In the weaving workshop, Albers assisted in dyeing yarns and made her first wall hangings and yard fabrics. She and her fellow

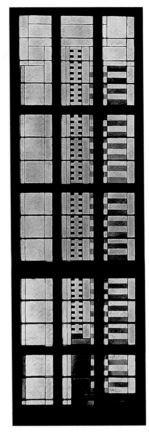

students participated in the first official Bauhaus exhibition in 1923, furnishing the experimental Haus am Horn with textiles.

Albers's first published writing appeared in 1924, as part of Gropius's drive to elicit public support for the Bauhaus. In it, she wrote: *The Bauhaus attempts to give the house what it needs today—functional form. . . . Its goals are the clear structure of things, suitable materials, and a new type of beauty. This new beauty is not style. . . . Today a thing is beautiful when its form is in agreement with its function, and when it has been made of well-chosen materials.*[14]

1925–26

In 1925, three years after Albers first met Josef Albers at the Bauhaus in Weimar, they were married. By that time Josef had advanced rapidly at the school, from student in the glass workshop to instructor of the Vorkurs in 1923, and to junior Bauhaus Master in 1925. They traveled to Italy for their honeymoon.

"It was in the . . . few years after their wedding that their art work bore the closest resemblance. . . . Each was responding to new possibilities of abstraction, to the idea of playfulness with the figure-ground relationship, to the comforts afforded by control. Right angles, solid expanses of color, and pure bands of black became part of their new language."[15]

That same year the Bauhaus moved from Weimar to its new Modernist glass-walled structure in Dessau, designed by Gropius. But the aesthetic harmony that Gropius imagined would flourish

189. Josef Albers in his studio at the Bauhaus, Dessau, 1929, photographed by Umbo.

190. Anni and Josef Albers on a balcony of the Bauhaus building, Dessau, ca. 1926, photographed by Marianne Brandt.

191. Josef Albers, stained-glass window, Ullstein Printing Works, Templehof, Berlin, 1927.

192. Josef Albers, *Anni Sommer '23*, 1923.
Collage of two photographs,
mounted on cardboard, 29.7 x 41.7 cm
(11 ¹⁵⁄₁₆ x 16 ⅛ inches).
The Josef and Anni Albers Foundation,
Bethany JAF: PH-423.

at the Bauhaus proved to be an elusive goal.

Concerned with form and with the shape of objects surrounding us—that is, with design—we will have to look at the things we have made. With the evidence of our work before us, we cannot escape its verdict. Today it tells us of separateness, of segregation and fragmentation, if I interpret rightly.

For here we find two distinct points of departure: the scientific and technological, and the artistic. Too often these approaches arrive at separate results instead of at a single, all-inclusive form that embodies the whole of our needs: the need for the functioning of a thing and the need for an appearance that responds to our sense of form.[16]

In 1926 Albers began to work on the double and jacquard looms. Color illustrations of her

wall hangings were published in the German journal *Offset* and in *Tapis et Tissus*, a portfolio selected by Sonia Delaunay.[17]

In Dessau, the Bauhaus's focus shifted from craft to production.

A most curious change took place when the idea of a practical purpose, a purpose aside from the purely artistic one, suggested itself to this group of weavers. Such a thought, ordinarily in the foreground, had not occurred to them, having been so deeply absorbed in the problems of the material itself and the discoveries of unlimited ways of handling it. This consideration of usefulness brought about a profoundly different conception. A shift took place from the free play with forms to a logical building of structures.[18]

Women students occupied an ambiguous space at the Bauhaus. "[In] the widening polarization between industry and craft . . .

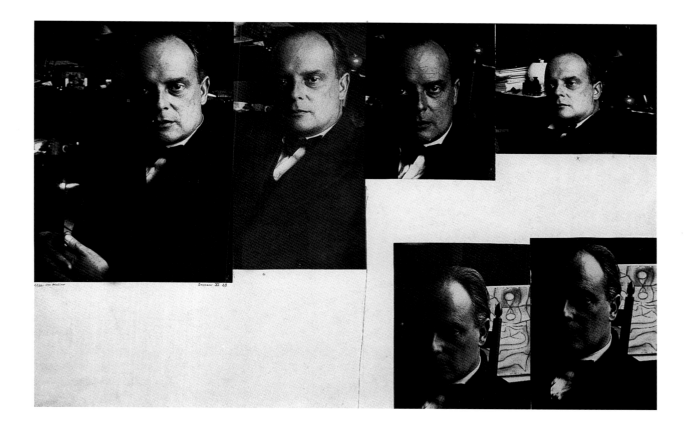

women were identified with the latter. As mechanization and industrialization increased, the role of the designer gained in status and attracted males. Women lost ground. . . . The ambivalence of the weavers is nowhere better expressed than in their own writing."[19]

It is interesting . . . to observe that in ancient myths from many parts of the world it was a goddess, a female deity, who brought the invention of weaving to mankind. When we realize that weaving is primarily a process of structural organization this thought is startling, for today thinking in terms of structure seems closer to the inclination of men than women. . . . Later, with weaving traditions established, embellishing as one of the weaver's tasks moved to the foreground and thus the feminine role in it has become natural in our eyes.[20]

1927–32

In 1927 the weaving workshop students asked Paul Klee to teach a class in design. Klee developed a program specifically geared toward weaving, which he taught until 1931, when he resigned from the Bauhaus. "Klee's repeated insistence that the ultimate form of a work was not as important as the process leading to it . . . aimed at inculcating a specific way of perceiving the world. It proposed to the student what Klee himself believed and made the basis of his work: that the wellsprings of human and natural creation are essentially one; that art and science have their roots in the selfsame order of things. . . . The process Klee taught, while rationalistic, was ultimately nonrational."[21]

Although Albers revered Klee, she later admitted, *One of his classes was so far over my head that I didn't understand anything and*

193. Josef Albers, *Klee im Atelier, Dessau XI '29*, 1929. Collage of six photographs, mounted on cardboard, 29.7 x 41.7 cm (11 ¹¹⁄₁₆ x 16 ⅛ inches). The Josef and Anni Albers Foundation, Bethany JAF: PH-2.

194, 195, and 196. Josef and Anni Albers, Dessau, ca. 1925.

197. Anni and Josef Albers, Oberstdorf, Germany, 1927–28.

198. Josef and Anni Albers, ca. 1935.

had to leave. I was not yet ready for Klee and his thinking.[22]

Also in 1927 Albers designed wall coverings and curtains for the Theater Café Altes in Dessau and the curtain for a theater in Oppeln. These projects required new approaches.

It is really interesting to concentrate like an architect has to concentrate on the functioning of a house, so I enjoyed concentrating on what [a] specific material demanded. I developed a series of wall-covering materials, which at the time I did it was nonexistent really. And I tried to make them so that they were partly even light-reflecting, that they could be brushed off, that they could be fixed straight and easily on the wall without pulling into different shapes. So a specific task sets you a very interesting way of dealing with your choice of material, with your technique.[23]

In July 1927 the Alberses took a trip to the Canary Islands. *I was always the one who thought*

of [travel] when we were still at the Bauhaus—and married not for a very long time. This was wonderful to be away from the parents' choice of vacations—when we always went to Bavaria to winter in one of the wettest corners, Oberstdorf. And I thought [instead] sun and sea and so on. I found a banana boat and we went to Tenerife, to the Canaries. . . . It was such a small boat and it took three weeks to go there. It was quite shaky and there were only twelve people.[24]

Despite Albers's dislike of Oberstdorf, she and Josef did vacation there in the winter of 1927–28. Albers's sister, Lotte, recalled, "I went twenty-four times to Oberstdorf in Bavaria. . . . It was what you did for four weeks every year—you took the cook and the governess and lived in a peasant house. The peasants moved out to the barn. . . . Anni didn't like to go climbing—she would stay at home and paint and read."[25]

In 1928 Gropius left the Bauhaus to return to private architectural practice, and Hannes Meyer, a Swiss architect, took his place. Herbert Bayer, Marcel Breuer, and Lucia and László Moholy-Nagy resigned in the wake of Gropius's departure. The Alberses moved into the master's house vacated by the Moholy-Nagys and became neighbors of the Klees and the Kandinskys. Albers became an assistant in the weaving workshop under Stölzl's direction, and from September to December the following year and again in the fall of 1931 she replaced Stölzl as acting director.

In the 1929 summer recess, the Alberses traveled to Avignon, Geneva, Biarritz, and Paris and in August to Barcelona for the International Exposition, where Ludwig Mies van der Rohe and Lilly Reich had designed the German exhibits.

Also in 1929 Albers designed a wall-covering material for the new auditorium of the Allgemeinen Deutschen Gewerkschaftsbundes-schule in Bernau, for which Meyer was the architect.

Hannes Meyer was building a large school . . . and in the auditorium there was an echo. . . . And he asked me if I could think of a way of subduing this echo, if we could make a textile that would be suitable. The usual solution at that time in the '20s was that you put velvet on the walls. The little fibers absorbed the sound. And of course if the velvet was to be at all practical in a room used by hundreds of people so very often it would have to be a dark color. Otherwise you could see all the marks of fingerprints and so on. . . .

And I had an idea that if I made a surface that was made out of a kind of cellophane—and cellophane just was coming in as a new material—we had been in Florence, Italy, and I had bought a little crocheted cap made of this

199. Josef and Anni Albers (rear center) with Bauhaus friends, ca. 1925.

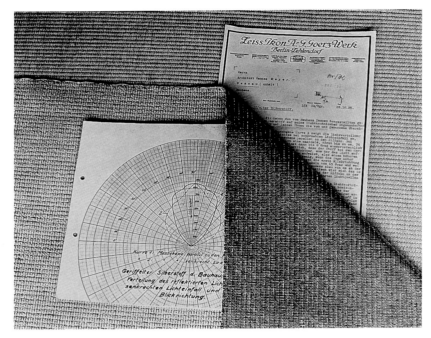

200. Walter Gropius, 1930, photographed by Josef Albers.

201. Wall-covering material for the auditorium of the Allgemeinen Deutschen Gewerkschaftsbundesschule, Bernau, Germany, 1929 (see cat. no. 127), showing the reverse side with label indicating the reflection of light as analyzed by Zeiss Ikon, Berlin.

material. And I unraveled it and used it for the first attempt . . . and this velvet quality of absorption I put in an interesting construction into the back of this material. So it had on the surface a light-reflecting quality and in the back the sound-absorbing quality.

And this went into production. I don't think it was made on machines, but it was made in workshops that made yard goods. And it was used for this auditorium. And it worked. . . . And the Zeiss Ikon Works in Germany made a kind of analysis of how the light-reflecting surface worked. . . . So this was quite an intriguing kind of textile engineering.[26]

Albers later said of this material that it was *something I am really happy to sign with my name, for that was a completely new approach.*[27]

Albers was awarded her Bauhaus diploma for the wall-covering material for the Bernau

auditorium in 1930. The same year two of Albers's works were shown in *Ausstellung Moderner Bildwirkereien*, an exhibition of Modern textiles. During the summer she traveled with Josef to San Sebastián, Spain, and to the Tyrol, Ascona, and Lake Maggiore in Italy. Their travels are documented in Josef's photographs. In August 1930 Mies van der Rohe replaced Meyer as director of the Bauhaus, and appointed Reich as the new director of the weaving workshop.

At the important *Deutsche Bauausstellung* (German building exhibition) in Berlin in July 1931, Albers's work was awarded the Stadt Berlin Prize.

In October 1932 the Bauhaus was forced to close in Dessau after the National Socialist party came to power in the local government and cut funding to the school. Mies van der Rohe reopened the school as a private institution in Berlin, and for the next six

Germans To Teach Art Near Here

Professor Josef and Frau Albers, above, of Dessau, Germany, where they taught art in the famous Bauhaus school there until Hitler's policies caused it to close recently, this week joined the faculty of Black Mountain college at Blue Ridge to conduct an art department in the college.

Germans On Faculty At Black Mountain School

Josef And Frau Albers Named Instructors In Art There

With Professor Josef and Frau Albers, of Dessau, Germany, as instructors, an art department has been established at Black Mountain college at Blue Ridge near here.

Professor and Frau Albers were until recently members of the faculty of the Bauhaus school in Des-

sau, which was world famous as an exponent of the international idea of art. The school was forced to close because of the national educational policies of the new Hitler government. The two art teachers were brought to Black Mountain college, the only college in the United States under direct faculty control, by the New York Museum of Art.

Internationally Known

Having served as an instructor of art at the Bauhaus school for the last decade, Professor Albers is internationally known in modern art

months—during which time the Alberses moved to Berlin, where they lived in an apartment at 28 Sensenburgerallee in the suburb of Charlottenburg—it operated from a disused factory building in the Steiglitz neighborhood. On April 11, 1933, the school was again forced to close after the National Socialists gained control of the national government. Mies van der Rohe protested and obtained official consent to reopen the school four months later, but the conditions that accompanied this permission were so onerous that on August 10, 1933, he announced the decision of the faculty to close the school officially and finally. "Anni at age thirty-four and her husband at age forty-five were suddenly without jobs and had little hope of continuing their work in an atmosphere rapidly becoming hostile to abstract art."[28]

1933–36

As the Bauhaus was forced to close, Black Mountain College, a new, small, experimental college, near Asheville, North Carolina, was searching for someone to head its art program. Philip Johnson and Edward M.M. Warburg, both fledgling curators at the new Museum of Modern Art in New York, learned of this through Theodore (Ted) Dreier, one of the school's founders. Johnson and Warburg had both visited the Dessau Bauhaus, and Johnson was in Berlin in the summer of 1933.

Philip Johnson, who now has a very great name, then we knew as a somewhat spoiled, interesting student from Harvard. . . . He . . . was in Berlin . . . and I had made experiments with different materials, strawlike materials. . . . He was visiting Lilly Reich, who . . . was practically in charge of the weaving workshop. . . . Philip was there [at Lilly Reich's apartment], and he was shown materials, and somehow

202. *Asheville Citizen*, December 5, 1933.

203. Josef and Anni Albers on the steps of their living quarters at the Blue Ridge Campus of Black Mountain College, ca. 1937.

204. Anni Albers, Black Mountain College, ca. 1935.

205. Josef Albers on the deck outside the dining hall at the Lake Eden campus of Black Mountain College, ca. 1935.

206. Student dance on the verandah of Robert E. Lee Hall at the Blue Ridge campus of Black Mountain College, ca. 1937, photographed by Josef Albers.

in the doorway I met him at Lilly Reich's, and I said, "Oh, you are here. Would you be interested in coming to a cup of tea with us? I would love to show you also some of my things." And he came in the afternoon and I put out my wall hangings. They were all big, and they all had to do with practical ideas, strawlike material that could be brushed off or cleaned in some specific way, and with various transparencies and so on.

And he looked at them and said, "Now who made them? I saw these at Lilly Reich's."

And I said, "No, they are mine."

And he said, "But she never told me about that." . . .

And in the door when he left, he said, "Would you like to come to America?"

And it was just the high time for us to leave. For instance, the Bauhaus was closed. I had the wrong kind of background in Hitler's ideas and so on and we said, "Well,

of course." And it was after six weeks we got a letter asking us to come to this newly founded college.[29]

On August 17, 1933, Johnson wrote to the Alberses, inviting them, on behalf of the trustees of Black Mountain College, to come to the United States. Warburg agreed to fund their steamship tickets. Johnson recalls, "It was the combination of Eddie knowing about Black Mountain and the idea that the Alberses might want to come to America to work. . . . So I said, 'Let's get them over.' It seemed the most natural thing in the world. I think he [Eddie] paid all the money out."[30] The couple arrived in New York on the S.S. Europa on November 24, 1933. Josef wrote to Kandinsky, "We were met by four Bauhaus colleagues. We were twelve hours late. Four hotels had been booked.

207 and 208. Anni Albers in the cornfields, Black Mountain College, ca. 1937.

Four journalists were waiting to interview us. First night dinner at the Dreiers' . . . with Miss Katherine Dreier. Very lively. . . . Museum of Modern Art very good. Brancusi exhibition very beautiful. Arranged by Duchamp who we met on this occasion. A wonderful person."[31]

Albers spoke to the press on behalf of Josef, who was not conversant in English: *He says that in this country at last he will find a free atmosphere. . . . He says that art must have freedom in which to grow, and that is no longer possible in Germany. There a professor must teach only the art that the government thinks is forwarding the German ideal of government.*[32]

The New York Sun reported: "Tall, slim and vivacious, Frau Albers looks more like a student than like the leader of a movement, and speaks English slowly and solemnly much as a child recites a poem 'by heart.' . . . Today she is known not only for the uniqueness of her designs, which are woven directly 'into the material' but for her experiments with materials.' It is not enough that textiles should be pretty!', she exclaimed, looking almost fearfully at the somewhat lavish tapestries of the hotel lounge. 'Most commercial houses take their designs off the paper, *nicht*? with no regard for the fitness of that design for a given place. We of Bauhaus are not hostile to industry but we create patterns close to the materials and at the same time related to the use of the textile.'"[33]

Speaking of the Alberses' arrival at Black Mountain, Barbara (Bobbie) Dreier, wife of Ted Dreier, recalls that Josef "had Thanksgiving dinner with my husband's parents in Brooklyn Heights the night before. They put him on the train with his nice wife and . . . they

209. Anni Albers with Ted and Bobbie
Dreier en route to Florida and Cuba, 1935.

came. We settled them in and they
adjusted to the completely different life that they found there in this
great big Robert E. Lee Hall."[34]

We arrived on November 24,
I think, 1933. Just when the
Chancellery in Germany burned
and everything was in ruins . . . and
then we were not knowing very
much. . . . And so we got there and
after three or four days . . . there was
a big festival at the college, which
had only fifty or sixty students, . . . a
great event that was Thanksgiving.
And we thought it was really a day to
be thankful for and we celebrated it.[35]

Albers was appointed Assistant
Professor of Art, and Josef was
appointed Professor of Art.

It was interesting to see a new
life, and interesting to see a professor
with a hammer in his hand. This
didn't exist in Europe. There a profes-
sor was a professor.[36]

"Drawing upon the early
Bauhaus model, Albers promoted a
teaching method of 'playful pro-
ductivity.' She felt that students

progress from unencumbered
experimentation with materials . . .
to work that serves functional or
aesthetic ends."[37] "Although there
were similar weaving programs at
the Institute of Design, Cranbrook
Academy of Art, and the Art
Institute of Chicago, the Black
Mountain program produced
distinctive textiles. Exhibited
throughout the United States, they
were recognized for their emphasis
on the thread rather than purely
coloristic or textural effects and
for their limited range of colors,
primarily black, white, and natural
fibers. They reflected Anni Albers's
aesthetic that 'textiles are serving
objects that should be modest
in appearance and blend into the
background.'"[38]

The Alberses rapidly became
part of the Black Mountain College
community. "Black Mountain
wunderbar," Albers wrote in
a letter dated December 3, 1933,

210 and 211. Bobbie Dreier and Anni Albers, 1935.

carbon copies of which were received by several of their friends in Germany.[39]

Barely a year later, in December 1934, Josef was invited to lecture in Cuba. Bobbie Dreier recalls, "Clarita Porcet . . . had invited them to go to Cuba, and we offered to drive them down [to Florida]. . . . We had a sort of a Christmas vacation [and then] we took them all the way to Key West to put them on a boat. And they said, 'Well, why don't you come, for goodness sake? We can take the car over and everything.' And we went."[40] "When in 1934 the Alberses drove through Florida with their new good friends Theodore and Barbara Dreier en route to Havana, it occurred to Anni, that the two couples might venture toward the source of [Pre-Columbian] art and travel to Mexico the following year."[41]

In the summer of 1935 the Alberses made the first of fourteen visits to Mexico, traveling to Oaxaca and Acapulco with Ted and Bobbie in the Dreiers' secondhand Model A convertible.

We have had a wonderful summer here in Mexico. . . . we arrived here in our car after traveling for seven days, at times through high mountains. Mexico City is at an altitude of 2,300 meters, so even though it is so far south it is marvelously cool, a truly refreshing climate. And a country for art, like no other, wonderful ancient art, barely yet discovered . . . and much new art, frescoes: you surely know Rivera, Orosco [sic], and others, then Merida, the talented abstract painter, Crespo—art is the most important thing in this country. Imagine that.[42]

They became collectors of Pre-Columbian art:
During our many trips to Mexico— fourteen in all, some of three months' duration and dating back as far as 1936 [sic]—we had gathered here and there material covering some

212. Anni Albers and her father, Siegfried Fleischmann, Mexico, 1937, photographed by Josef Albers.

of the diverse early cultures of this ancient country. Our first small pieces came to us on our visits to prehistoric sites from little boys offering them to us through the car window, just as turkeys and goats were also held up for sale. As we examined the fragments of pottery, which included subtly formed heads and, alas, usually broken figurines, we could not believe that here in our hands were century-old Pre-Columbian pieces found by the peasants when plowing their fields. We showed our little treasures to the late George Valliant, the authority on Mexican archaeology, who was excavating at the time on the outskirts of Mexico City, and he confirmed their authenticity. Yes, here was a country whose earth still yielded such art.[43]

1937–38

In 1937 the Alberses put together an exhibition of Mayan art at Black Mountain College.

On March 17 of that year Albers went to New York and met Walter and Ise Gropius as they arrived in the United States. (Walter Gropius was taking up an appointment at the Graduate School of Design at Harvard University, Cambridge, Massachusetts.)

Albers's parents arrived in Veracruz, Mexico, on June 18, meeting the Alberses (who were on their third Mexican trip) in Mexico City the following day. Toni Fleischmann wrote in her diary, "Now I am eagerly looking forward to Anke [Anni] and Jup [Josef]. Tomorrow at last we will see each other again after almost four years!"[44] For the next month the Alberses introduced Anni's parents to the major sites in Mexico: "June 23. We drive to the Tenayuca Pyramid. . . . Juppi and Pap again buy small heads of gods, which are still being discovered,

and they cost only a few cents."[45] After the Fleischmanns departed to return to Berlin via New York, Albers's mother wrote: "Farewells quite difficult. Who knows when we will see each other again. Juppis [Toni's nickname for Anni and Josef] were touching, so concerned about everything, and marvelous all the things they showed us."[46]

The following year Albers helped the Gropiuses and Herbert Bayer assemble material for the exhibition *Bauhaus 1919–1928* at the Museum of Modern Art in New York. Albers's weavings were included in the exhibition, and she contributed the essay "The Weaving Workshop" to the exhibition catalogue.[47] Another article, "Work with Material," was published in the leaflet "Black Mountain College, Bulletin 5" in November.[48]

1939

Albers became a United States citizen on May 17, 1939, and Josef did likewise on December 12. In June they traveled to Mexico again for Josef to teach at Gobers College in Tlalpan. Albers's parents, forced to flee Germany, set out for Mexico once more. Josef wrote to Bayer, "We plan to go to Mexico about June 3 to meet Anni's parents, who are moving there, unless a European explosion intervenes."[49] Toni Fleischmann reported, "In 1937 I wrote a diary about our first trip to Mexico and I never imagined that I would see that country again. Now, two years later to the day, we begin the same journey on the same boat, the 'Orinoco,' but under totally different circumstances. At that time it was a trip to see our children again and through them to see a distant and lovely country. Today it is a departure from our native land, which we must leave forever."[50] Albers wrote of the

213. Anni Albers and her parents, Siegfried and Toni Fleischmann, Teotihuacán, Mexico, 1937, photographed by Josef Albers.

214 and 215. Anni Albers at the loom and with a student, Black Mountain College, ca. 1937.

trip to Mexico to meet her parents: *Our trip was fine. . . . We have seen all ready [sic] quite a lot; one pyramid, one market, one fresco, and last night had our first party; with painters and Americans and all of it a little crazy. . . . Rivera who was supposed to come was not there, naturally. We expect my family sometime next week and plan to drive down to Vera Cruz [sic] to meet them.[51]*

1940–49

In the 1940s Albers began to make small-scale weavings, which she mounted on linen bases and framed.

I developed there [at Black Mountain College] gradually these what I call "pictorial weavings." Which was really not what the Bauhaus was meant to do. . . . Gropius never quite forgave me that I went into the art side. . . . It was the one thing that gradually made me a little more known. . . . It was [an] inventive use of new materials and constructions that had not been used in many centuries. . . . [Josef] wasn't terribly interested in textiles. But he thought that it was nice that I did something.[52]

Her weavings were exhibited widely in the 1940s, and she was in demand as a teacher, a lecturer, and a writer during this time.[53] In an article that drew caustic responses from traditional handweavers, Albers stated that handweaving should be seen

216 and 217. Anni Albers, ca. 1937, photographed by Josef Albers.

as more than "a romantic attempt to recall a 'temps perdu'":

If conceived as a preparatory step to machine production the work will be more than the revival of a lost skill and will take responsible part in a new development.[54]

In the spring of 1941 the Alberses went to Harvard, where Josef taught at the Graduate School of Design.

On May 5 of that year an exhibition of jewelry that Albers had made with a student, Alex Reed, from curtain rings, hairpins, paper clips, bottle caps, glass drawer knobs, clay insulators, metal washers, and other household items, opened at the Willard Gallery in New York. The exhibition traveled to the Katherine Kuh Gallery, Chicago; the Addison Gallery of American Art, Andover, Massachusetts; the Fitchburg Art Center, Fitchburg, Massachusetts; and the Museum of Art, Smith College, Northampton, Massachusetts. Many of the pieces were sold. One reviewer exclaimed: "Modern times have produced a number of new and sometimes strange things. But 'til now we'd never heard of utilizing electricians' supplies, bathroom fixtures, plumbers' accessories, and a hardware merchant's stock to make— JEWELRY!

"Maybe it's another of those things brought on by conserving what we have. . . . And . . . it's proving 'smart.' . . . It comes from the hands of Anni Albers, exponent of Art in the Black Mountain School [sic] of North Carolina . . . a fertile imagination seems to be the main requisite for its creation. . . .

"One of the most interesting pieces . . . was a plaque formed by using a perforated sink strainer at the end of a shower curtain chain and hanging a fringe of paper clips from the lower edge of it!"[55]

The jewelry was included in *Modern Handmade Jewelry*, an exhibition organized by the

Museum of Modern Art in New York and shown there and at fifteen other museums across the country beginning in 1946. Albers wrote to the exhibition's organizer, Jane Sabersky, from New Mexico: *Of course you can keep our necklaces for further exhibitions. Glad to learn it is a success. We found the perfect place to rent and quick, with marvelous food too. We will stay here until spring and then continue into Old Mexico.*[56]

Around 1944 Philip Johnson commissioned drapery material from Albers for the Rockefeller guest house on East Fifty-second Street in New York. Albers chose the unusual combination of cotton chenille with white plastic and copper foil to create a curtain with a calm appearance during the day that transformed into a sparkling surface at night.

The Alberses traveled less between 1940 and 1945, possibly because they could no longer go to Mexico after it allied itself with

Germany in 1942. After the war, however, they returned to Mexico, taking an extended sabbatical from October 1946 to November 1947 and traveling there via Canada, the Midwest, California, Texas, and New Mexico. In El Paso, Albers was hospitalized for several weeks and underwent surgery. She recuperated in La Luz, New Mexico, and celebrated her recovery in the pictorial weaving *La Luz I.*

The utopia of Black Mountain College began to falter, and Josef, who reluctantly agreed to be rector in October 1948, resigned from that position on March 14, 1949. At the end of the semester the Alberses left Black Mountain College for the last time and traveled to Mexico City, where Josef taught at the University of Mexico. In August they moved to New York.

Edgar Kaufmann, Jr., director of the Department of Industrial Design at the Museum of Modern

Art in New York, had come to Black Mountain College in 1948 to lecture on design at the Summer Institute. *And he saw some of my things. . . . And he said, "Wouldn't you like to show your things at the Museum of Modern Art?" . . . And it turned out the museum was ready to do that . . . and I was the only textile person they had ever shown.*[57]

Albers met with Philip Johnson at the museum to discuss the exhibition on January 14, 1949. Johnson recalls, "As far as I had an interest in textiles it was all her [Albers]. And I took Alfred [Alfred H. Barr, director of the Museum of Modern Art] seriously . . . that he wanted . . . a total picture of the arts. I said, 'You cannot leave out textiles.' . . . So I plugged the idea of doing a textile show." [59] The exhibition, *Anni Albers Textiles*, which was held from September 13 to October 30, 1949, was the first presentation of the work of a single textile artist to be shown at the museum. It included studies of textures, small experimental textile samples, yard materials, pictorial weavings, and hanging screens. From 1950–53 the exhibition traveled to twenty-six museums in the United States and Canada.

I was very happy with the way [Johnson] took on my exhibition. . . . [It] showed mainly also things that were at one time of great interest to me. And that was using materials that usually were not used for textiles. I used synthetics and plastic materials. . . . And also I had the idea of making materials that are usually not existent, that is, partitions in rooms, rather transparent ones. . . . I made six or eight different transparencies.[60]

Of Albers's involvement, Johnson remembers: "I felt she wasn't a person to do a lot of P.R. And she'd always need help in that regard."[61]

219. Anni Albers, 1935, photographed by Josef Albers.

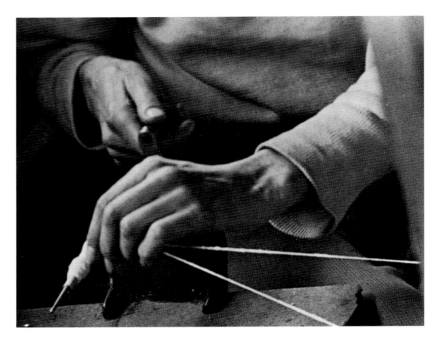

220 and 221. Anni Albers at her loom, 1943.

1950–59

In 1950 Josef was appointed chairman of the Department of Design of Yale University and the Alberses moved to New Haven, Connecticut. At their home, at 8 North Forest Circle, Albers played the role of housewife as well as artist for the first time. Responding to a commission from Gropius for his Harvard Law School building, she created bedspreads and partitions for the dormitories.

One of the materials was done in quite a great quantity. It was a black and white one, with jute. . . . Gropius . . . had the idea that it should be very masculine. . . . They had to be heavy . . . and have this strong structure so that you didn't see immediately, "Oh, he didn't wipe his feet, and here is a cigarette hole from Frank from last year still." . . . So I like to be on the practical side.[62]

Charles Sawyer, Dean of the Yale School of Art at the time, observed in 1995: "It was ironic in a way that Harvard was giving her more recognition as a creative artist than Yale. . . . In all candor, I don't think Josef was entirely sympathetic to her concerns. And I think he could have been."

Albers continued her experiments with textiles for production, and worked with the manufacturer Knoll on the realization of her designs as yard materials. The majority of her pictorial weavings (twenty-four of the thirty-six known works) were made during this decade, and she taught at art schools across the United States.

I was often asked here, at Yale, to give a few seminars to the architectural students. And what intrigued me in regard to teaching was that I think something should be reversed in teaching. We always, in architecture, or whatever you do, you start from what there is today and try to explain it. While I was trying to set

174

a task, put the students on absolute zero, in the desert, in Peru. Nothing is there. What is the first thing you have to think of? And build up? And maybe, for instance, something for fishing, or something for the roof. You gradually develop something, inventions, as you go along. . . . And some of the students . . . like also the idea of not being told a brick is done like this, and we build it like this, but how we arrive at the brick, you know?[63]

During the 1950s, the Alberses returned several times to Latin America, traveling to Mexico and Cuba in 1952 and to Peru and Chile in 1953 and 1956. In 1954 they traveled to Hawaii, where Josef taught at the University of Honolulu and Albers had an exhibition of her weavings at the Honolulu Academy of Arts. Also in 1954 Albers accompanied Josef to Ulm, Germany, where he gave a course in design at the new Hochschule für Gestaltung.

In January 1957 Albers's ark panels for Temple Emanu-El in Dallas, her first synagogue commission, were installed.

"The Pliable Plane: Textiles in Architecture," a lengthy article by Albers based on her work designing textiles for industry, appeared in *Perspecta*, a journal published by the Yale School of Architecture, in 1957.[64] *On Designing*, a compilation of Albers's writings, was published by Pellango Press in New Haven in 1959.

Also in 1959 the exhibition *Anni Albers, Pictorial Weavings* was presented by the Massachusetts Institute of Technology, Cambridge, Massachusetts, before it traveled to the Carnegie Institute of Technology, Pittsburgh; Baltimore Museum of Art; Yale University Art Gallery, New Haven, Connecticut; and Contemporary Arts Museum, Houston.

222. Josef and Anni Albers in Anni's workroom at 8 North Forest Circle, New Haven, Connecticut, ca. 1955.

223. Josef and Anni Albers, Monte Albán, Mexico, 1952.

224. Josef and Anni Albers at 8 North Forest Circle, New Haven, Connecticut, 1968, photographed by Henri Cartier-Bresson.

1960–69

In 1961 Albers received a second synagogue commission, for ark panels for Congregation B'nai Israel, Woonsocket, Rhode Island.

A commission for a work that is to be part of a building devoted to worship is a most gratifying one. For, though any work we do is an attempt to relate ourselves to something meaningful in a general sense, it is a source of special satisfaction to be able to participate in a task directed toward something we hold in reverence.[65]

That same year the American Institute of Architects recognized the significance of Albers's work within their profession and honored her with the AIA's Craftsmanship Medal.

Although she would continue to work at her loom for a few more years, in 1963 Albers turned, almost by chance, to printmaking.

My great breakaway came when my husband . . . was asked to work at the Tamarind Lithographic Workshop in Los Angeles where I, as

a useless wife, was hanging around, until June Wayne, head of the workshop, asked me to try lithography myself. I found that in this medium the image of threads could project a freedom I never suspected.[66]

I began to think, after I made my first print, "Now, there is something open, interesting to follow." And I knew nothing of the technique. They supplied the technicians.[67]

Albers was invited back to Tamarind as a fellow in 1964 and produced *Line Involvements*, a portfolio of seven lithographs.

Once having discovered this new freedom, I was never able to let go. . . . I find that, when the work is made with threads, it's considered a craft; when it's on paper, it's considered art. . . . Prints gave me a greater freedom of presentation. The multiplication and exactness of the process of printmaking allow for broader exhibition and ownership of work. As a result, recognition comes more easily and happily, the longed-for pat on the shoulder.[68]

Albers had been commissioned to write an entry on hand-weaving for a new edition of the *Encyclopedia Britannica* published in 1963, and this became the first chapter of *On Weaving*, her treatise on "textile fundamentals and methods" published by Wesleyan University Press in 1965.

The following year she completed *Six Prayers*, a commemorative tapestry commissioned for the Jewish Museum in New York.

I used the threads themselves as a sculptor or painter uses his medium to produce a scriptural effect which would bring to mind sacred texts. . . . These panels are mounted on rigid backgrounds to produce the effect of commemorative stelae.[70]

1970–94

In 1970, when the Alberses moved to 808 Birchwood Drive in Orange, about ten miles from New Haven, Albers gave up weaving altogether in favor of printmaking. *I could not stand the idea anymore of all the yarns and looms. It took too long and it always produced just one piece. . . . I just outgrew it in some way. It annoyed me and I can't do it anymore. . . . And then I gave away all the looms and all the yarns.*[71]

An exhibition of Albers's work—her first major show in Europe—was shown at the Kunstmuseum in Düsseldorf and at the Bauhaus-Archiv, Berlin, in 1975.

She continued her experiments in printmaking, working with Ken Tyler (whom she knew from Tamarind) at Gemini G.E.L. in Los Angeles and later at Tyler Graphics in New York, and extending her techniques into screenprinting and etching.

During these years, until 1994, she was honored with degrees and

225. Josef Albers at 8 North Forest Circle, New Haven, Connecticut, 1968, photographed by Henri Cartier-Bresson.

226. Maximillian Schell and Anni Albers,
Yale University Art Gallery,
New Haven, Connecticut, 1978.

227. Anni Albers and her brother,
Hans Farman, and sister, Lotte Benfey,
on Albers's eighty-fifth birthday,
Bethany, Connecticut, 1984.

awards from numerous institutions, including honorary doctorates in fine arts from the Maryland Institute College of Art, Baltimore, in 1972; the Philadelphia College of Art in 1976; and the University of Hartford in 1979; and an honorary doctorate of law from York University, Toronto, in 1973.

In March 1976, just after his eighty-eighth birthday, Josef died in New Haven, Connecticut, and Albers began to assume considerable responsibility as the primary guardian of his legacy.

In 1977 the Brooklyn Museum presented *Anni Albers: Prints and Drawings*, a comprehensive exhibition of her works on paper.

Albers designed a range of fabrics for Sunar, a textile company, in the 1980s, that has remained in production ever since.

Despite her disavowal of feminism, the Women's Caucus for Art presented Albers with an award for outstanding achievement in 1980.

In 1981, the textile artist Jack Lenor Larsen referred to Albers as a "visionary" as he presented her with the American Craft Council Gold Medal in New York. She responded: *As to name calling, instead of visionary, I suggest experimenter.*[72]

In 1982, at a meeting of the College Art Association in New York, she participated with Louise Nevelson, John Cage, and five others on a panel entitled "The Art/Craft Connection: Material as a Metaphor." During the panel, she stated:

How do we choose our specific material, our means of communication? "Accidentally." Something speaks to us, a sound, touch, hardness or softness, it catches us and asks us to be formed. We are finding our language, and as we go along we learn to obey their rules and their

228. Anni Albers, Milan, 1984.

229. Anni Albers at the Royal College
of Art graduation ceremony
to accept an honorary doctorate,
London, June 29, 1990.

limits. . . . Students worry about choosing their way. I always tell them, "You can go anywhere from anywhere."[73]

Albers continued to travel, visiting Europe several times during these years. In 1983 she presided over the opening of the Josef Albers Museum in Bottrop, Germany, Josef's birthplace.

Connections, a portfolio of nine screenprints, some based on her earlier designs from the Bauhaus, was published in Milan by Fausta Squatriti Editore in 1984.

A retrospective exhibition, *The Woven and Graphic Art of Anni Albers*, was presented at the Renwick Gallery of the National Museum of American Art, Smithsonian Institution, Washington, D.C., in 1985 and traveled to the Yale University Art Gallery, New Haven, Connecticut, in 1986.

In December 1989, a selection of her textiles, pictorial weavings, drawings, and prints, together with a selection of Josef's work, was exhibited in *Josef and Anni Albers*, organized by Albers's close friend Maximillian Schell, at the Villa Stuck in Munich and subsequently at the Josef Albers Museum.

In 1990 Albers traveled to London to accept an honorary doctorate from the Royal College of Art. Also in 1990 she received an honorary doctorate from the Rhode Island School of Design, Providence.

Albers's work was again seen in the Museum of Modern Art in 1990, this time alongside works by one of her former Bauhaus colleagues, in the exhibition *Gunta Stölzl. Anni Albers*.

Anni Albers died in Orange, Connecticut, on May 9, 1994.

1. Nicholas Fox Weber, "Anni Albers to Date," in *The Woven and Graphic Art of Anni Albers* (exh. cat.; Washington, D.C.: Smithsonian Institution Press, 1985), p. 15.

2. Conversation with Hans and Betty Farman, Bethany, Conn., June 8, 1998.

3. Ibid.

4. Reminiscences by Lotte Benfey, recorded by her grandson Philip Benfey in the late 1970s; transcript in The Josef and Anni Albers Foundation archives, Bethany, Conn.

5. Maximillian Schell, interview with Anni Albers, Orange, Conn., Dec. 16, 1989; transcript in The Josef and Anni Albers Foundation archives.

6. Ibid.

7. Nicholas Fox Weber, "Anni Albers to Date," p. 16.

8. Savim Fesci, interview with Anni Albers, New Haven, Conn., July 5, 1968, Archives of American Art, New York; transcript in The Josef and Anni Albers Foundation archives.

9. Walter Gropius, *Programm des Staatlichen Bauhauses in Weimar* (Weimar, April 1919), p. 4.

10. Walter Gropius, letter to Annie Weil, Feb. 23, 1920, Weimar State Archives no. 259, 48; quoted in Anja Baumhoff, "Gender, Art and Handicraft at the Bauhaus," Ph.D. diss., Johns Hopkins University, Baltimore, 1994, p. 82.

11. Schell, interview with Albers, Dec. 16, 1989.

12. Sigrid Wortmann Weltge, interview with Anni Albers, Orange, Conn., Feb. 21, 1987; transcript in The Josef and Anni Albers Foundation archives.

13. Ibid.

14. Annelise Fleischmann, "Wohnökonomie," special Bauhaus supplement to *Neue Frauenkleidung und Frauenkultur* (Karlsruhe, 1924). Albers's second published article, "Bauhausweberei," appeared in a special Bauhaus number of the journal *Junge Menschen* 8 (Nov. 1924), p. 188.

15. Nicholas Fox Weber, "Anni und Josef Albers: Gemeinsames Leben, gemeinsame Arbeit," in Josef Helfenstein and Henriette Mentha, *Josef und Anni Albers, Europa und Amerika, Künstlerpaare—Künstlerfreunde* (exh. cat.; Bern: Kunstmuseum Bern, 1998), p. 31.

16. Anni Albers, "Design: Anonymous and Timeless" (1947), in *On Designing* (Middletown, Conn.: Wesleyan University Press, 1971), p. 2.

17. *Offset* 7 (1926). *Tapis et Tissus, Art International d'Aujourd'hui* 15 (1926), plates 17 and 19.

18. Anni Albers, "Weaving at the Bauhaus" (Sept. 1938, revised July 1959), in *On Designing*, p. 2.

19. Sigrid Wortmann Weltge, *Bauhaus Textiles* (London: Thames and Hudson, 1993), pp. 98–99.

20. Anni Albers, "The Pliable Plane: Textiles in Architecture," *Perspecta* 4 (1957), pp. 36–41; reprinted in *On Designing*, p. 19.

21. Marcel Franciscono, "Paul Klee in the Bauhaus: The Artist as Lawgiver," *Arts Magazine* 52 (Sept. 1977), pp. 122–27.

22. Weltge, interview with Albers, Feb. 21, 1987.

23. Fesci, interview with Albers, July 5, 1968.

24. Schell, interview with Albers, Dec. 16, 1989.

25. Reminiscences by Lotte Benfey, late 1970s.

26. Fesci, interview with Albers, July 5, 1968.

27. Weltge, interview with Albers, Feb. 21, 1987.

28. Weber, "Anni Albers to Date," p. 20.

29. Schell, interview with Albers, Dec. 16, 1989.

30. Nicholas Fox Weber and Pandora Tabatabai Asbaghi, interview with Philip Johnson, New Canaan, Conn., July 26, 1998.

31. Josef Albers, letter to Vasily Kandinsky, Dec. 12, 1933, in *Kandinsky–Albers: Une Correspondance des années trente* (Paris: Centre Pompidou, 1998), p. 17.

32. "Art Professor, Fleeing Nazis, Here to Teach," *Brooklyn Daily Eagle*, Nov. 26, 1933, p. 8A.

33. "One of Germany's Foremost Textile Designers Comes Here to Teach in Southern Mountain School," *New York Sun*, Dec. 4, 1933, p. 34.

34. Frederick A. Horowitz, interview with Barbara (Bobbie) Dreier, June 14, 1996; transcript in The Josef and Anni Albers Foundation archives.

35. Schell, interview with Albers, Dec. 16, 1989.

36. Richard Polsky, interview with Anni Albers, Orange, Conn., Jan. 11, 1985, "American Craftspeople Project," Oral Research Office, Columbia University, New York; transcript in The Josef and Anni Albers Foundation archives, p. 35.

37. Mary Jane Jacob, "Anni Albers: A Modern Weaver as Artist," in *The Woven and Graphic Art of Anni Albers* (Washington, D.C.: Smithsonian Institution Press, 1985), p. 67.

38. Mary Emma Harris, *The Arts at Black Mountain College* (Cambridge, Mass.: MIT Press, 1987), p. 24.

39. Copies of this letter are in The Josef and Anni Albers Foundation archives.

40. Nicholas Fox Weber, telephone conversation with Bobbie Dreier, July 29, 1998.
41. Nicholas Fox Weber, preface, in Karl Taube, *The Josef and Anni Albers Collection of Pre-Columbian Art* (New York: Hudson Hills Press, 1988), p. 9.
42. Anni Albers, letter to Vasily and Nina Kandinsky, Aug. 22, 1936, in *Kandinsky–Albers: Une Correspondance des années trente*, p. 77.
43. Anni Albers, *Pre-Columbian Mexican Miniatures: The Josef and Anni Albers Collection* (New York: Praeger, 1970), unpaginated.
44. Toni Ullstein Fleischmann, travel diary, June 17, 1937; English transcript, translated by Fleischmann's grandson Theodor Benfey, in The Josef and Anni Albers Foundation archives.
45. Ibid.
46. Ibid., July 16, 1937.
47. Anni Albers, "The Weaving Workshop," in Walter Gropius, Ise Gropius, and Herbert Bayer, *Bauhaus 1919–1928* (exh. cat.; New York: Museum of Modern Art, 1938, 1952), pp. 141–42; revised in July 1959 and reprinted as "Weaving at the Bauhaus," in *On Designing*, pp. 38–40.
48. Reprinted in *College Art Journal* 3, no. 2 (Jan. 1944), pp. 51–54; and in *On Designing*, pp. 50–53.
49. Josef Albers, letter to Herbert Bayer, May 12, 1939; Black Mountain College Papers, North Carolina State Archives, Raleigh.
50. Toni Ullstein Fleischmann, "Thrown Off the Track" (1939), unpublished account of the Fleischmanns' emigration from Germany to the United States; English transcript, translated by Fleischmann's grandson Theodor Benfey, in The Josef and Anni Albers Foundation archives.
51. Anni Albers, letter to Anne Mangold, June 15, 1939; Black Mountain College Papers, North Carolina State Archives, Raleigh.
52. Schell, interview with Albers, Dec. 16, 1989.
53. Albers's publications in the 1940s were: "Designing," *Craft Horizons* 2, no. 2 (May 5, 1943), pp. 7–9; "We Need the Crafts for Their Contact with Materials," *Design* 46, no. 4 (Dec. 12, 1944), pp. 21–22 (reprinted as "One Aspect of Art Work," in *On Designing*, pp. 30–33); "Constructing Textiles," in Alvin Lustig, ed., *Visual Communication* (New York, 1945); reprinted in *Design* 47, no. 8 (April 4, 1946) and in *On Designing*, pp. 12–16; "Design: Anonymous and Timeless," *The Magazine of Art* 40, no. 2 (Feb. 1947), pp. 51–53 (reprinted in *On Designing*, pp. 1–9); "Fabrics," *Art and Architecture* 63 (March 1948), p. 33; and "Weavings," *Art and Architecture* 66 (Feb. 1949), p. 24.
54. Anni Albers, "Handweaving Today—Textile Work at Black Mountain College," *The Weaver* 6, no. 1 (Jan.–Feb. 1941), pp. 1–4. In response to this article, Mary M. Atwater, the originator of a popular home-weaving course, scoffed: "The making of models for industry—I fancy industry would consider this a big joke!" "It's Pretty—But Is It Art?" *The Weaver* 6, no. 3 (July–Aug. 1941), p. 13.
55. Dorothy Randall, "Hardware, Plumbing Gadgets Make Jewelry," *The Pittsburgh Sun-Telegraph,* Nov. 18, 1941.
56. Anni Albers, letter to Jane Sabersky, La Luz, New Mexico, Jan. 20, 1947; The Josef and Anni Albers Foundation archives.
57. Polsky, interview with Albers, Jan. 11, 1985, p. 28.
58. Report of meeting between Johnson and Albers, Jan. 14, 1949, exhibition files, Department of Architecture and Design, The Museum of Modern Art, New York.
59. Weber and Asbaghi, interview with Johnson, July 26, 1998.
60. Polsky, interview with Albers, Jan. 11, 1985; "The Reminiscences of Anni Albers," p. 29.
61. Weber and Asbaghi, interview with Johnson, July 26, 1998.
62. Polsky, interview with Albers, Jan. 11, 1985; "The Reminiscences of Anni Albers," pp. 31–32.
63. Ibid., pp. 17–18.
64. "The Pliable Plane: Textiles in Architecture," *Perspecta* 4 (1957), pp. 36–41.
65. Anni Albers, unpublished typewritten statement, June 1962; The Josef and Anni Albers Foundation archives.
66. Gene Baro, interview with Anni Albers, in *Anni Albers* (exh. cat.; New York: Brooklyn Museum, 1977), p. 7.
67. Polsky, interview with Albers, Jan. 11, 1985; "The Reminiscences of Anni Albers," p. 21.
68. Ibid.
69. Preface, *On Weaving* (Middletown, Conn.: Wesleyan University Press, 1965), p. 15.
70. Statement by Anni Albers in an undated press release issued by the Jewish Museum, New York; copy in The Josef and Anni Albers Foundation archives.
71. Schell, interview with Albers, Dec. 16, 1989.
72. Anni Albers, letter to Jack Lenor Larsen, July 23, 1981; The Josef and Anni Albers Foundation archives.
73. Transcript in The Josef and Anni Albers Foundation archives.

Photo credits (by figure number): 4, 21–23, 29, 39, 41–46, 49, 50, 53, 54, 56–58, 64–67, 132–47, 153–57, 161, 174, 175: Tim Nighswander; 5, 6: Die Neue Sammlung, Munich; 7, 38: Michael Nedzweski, ©President and Fellows of Harvard College, Harvard University, Cambridge, Mass.; 8, 9, 11–20, 40, 70–72, 83, 86–94, 107–18, 120–23, 125, 127, 156, 158–59, 160, 172, 180, 202, 218: ©1999 The Museum of Modern Art, New York; 10: David Mathews, ©President and Fellows of Harvard College, Harvard University, Cambridge, Mass.; 24, 25, 191: Bauhaus-Archiv GmbH, Berlin; 26, 30: ©ARS, New York; 27: Thomas Lunt, Department of Library Services, American Museum of Natural History, New York; 28: R.E. Logan, Department of Library Services, American Museum of Natural History, New York; 52, 68, 69, 73–82, 84, 85, 95–106, 119, 124, 126, 128–32, 158: ©1998 The Metropolitan Museum of Art, New York; 59: Lee Stalsworth; 60: John Parnell, ©The Jewish Museum, New York; 61–63: Ellen Labenski; 150, 164, 168: John Hill; 162, 163: BlackInk Architectural Photography, Dallas; 165, 223: Getulio Alviani; 171: Katherine Newbegin; 172, 201: Wide World Photos Inc.; 181: Faith Haacke; 189, 198: Research Library, Getty Research Institute, Los Angeles. Front cover: ©1998 The Metropolitan Museum of Art, New York.

Back cover: ©1947 Nancy Newhall. The Beaumont and Nancy Newhall estate. Courtesy of Scheinbaum and Russek Ltd.